Practice Problems for
C++ Beginners:
Moving Beyond the Basics

Kung-Hua Chang

Table of Contents

Preface

The first few practice examples were developed when I was a Ph.D. student in UCLA fulfilling my TA requirements in Fall 2012. The encouraging feedbacks from students have helped me to improve the practice examples while also retiring inadequate ones. After I received my Ph.D. in Computer Science, I had been a lecturer in UCLA teaching CS 32 about data structures in C++ over the summer of 2015 and 2016. At the very first class, I would always ask students to review the course materials from CS 31 - C++ programming, at the first week before they dive into the materials in CS 32 - data structures in C++. The original version of this book was made primarily for this purpose for students to review the course materials from CS 31 - C++ programming. By providing simple practice problems, students can quickly refresh their memory of the C++ syntax such as declaration of variables, control statements, loops, functions, pointers, pass-by-reference, and basic object-oriented programming. In order to make this book a better one, I have revised/revisited many practice problems from the original version of this book in Fall 2016 after I finished teaching the summer session in UCLA.

This book shall be treated as supplemental materials in addition to a formal introductory C++ book such as *Absolute C++*. This book should also be helpful to people who just started to learn C++ programming (not intended for intermediate / experienced C++ programmers though). I believe that using simple examples that hold important concepts helps people to learn C++ faster because many examples in a standard C++ textbook sometimes may be too complicated for C++ beginners to grab the important concepts behind them.

The practice examples in this book should **not** be viewed as examples of good coding styles. The practice examples were made with the intention to mislead novice programmers into thinking that a program should do this, but in actuality, the program does something else by utilizing bad coding styles or bad programming logic. The practice examples in this book are based on C++03 with some syntax from C++11. All the practice examples should be compiled successfully using Visual C++ 2015, and GCC 4.8.4 (except for those practice problems that were designed intentionally to cause compilation errors). Since the goal of this book is to make C++ beginners familiarize with the C++ syntax, only a few practice problems with source codes that are too long to type quickly by the readers have been uploaded to: https://github.com/KHC999/CS31 . Finally, the author hopes to use the proceeds from the sales of this book to establish a scholarship fund in UCLA.

Acknowledgements

I'd like to appreciate Professor David Smallberg from UCLA for his guidance on how to be a better lecturer. I'd also like to give my special thanks to Dr. Josiah L. Carlson for providing book title ideas.

Kung-Hua Chang, Ph.D.

Practice 1 – Variables and Operators

Problem 1.1: Does the following program compile successfully?

```cpp
#include <iostream>
using namespace std;

int main()
{
    int b;

    cin >> b;

    cout << B;
}
```

Problem 1.2: Does the following program compile successfully?

```cpp
#include <iostream>
using namespace std;

int main()
{
    double double;

    cin >> double;

    cout << double << endl;
}
```

Problem 1.3: Does the following program compile successfully?

```cpp
#include <iostream>
using namespace std;

int main()
{
    float float;

    cin >> float;

    cout << float << endl;
}
```

Problem 1.4. Please write a C++ program to print "C++" on the console.

Problem 1.5. Please write a C++ program to declare an integer variable x, take as an input an integer value and store such value to x, add 100 to x, and output x on the console.

Problem 1.6: Please use the variable X to fill in the blank to compute A, B, C, D, E as:

A = 4X
B = A / 100
C = A - B
D = A + 2B + 3C
E = A + B + C + D + X

If X is 5, then the outputs are:

20
0
20
80
125

```
#include <iostream>
using namespace std;

int main()
{
    int X, A, B, C, D, E;

    cin >> X ;

    A = _____

    B = _____

    C = _____

    D = _____

    E = _____

    cout << A << endl << B << endl << C << endl;
    cout << D << endl << E << endl;
}
```

Problem 1.7: What is the output of the program below?
```cpp
#include <iostream>
using namespace std;

int main()
{
    int G, I, V, E;

    G = I = V = E = 10;

    cout << G + I + V + E << endl;
}
```

Problem 1.8: What is the output of the program below?
```cpp
#include <iostream>
using namespace std;

int main()
{
    int Z;

    Z = (19 / 20) * 20;

    cout << Z << endl;
}
```

Problem 1.9: What is the output of the program below?
```cpp
#include <iostream>
using namespace std;

int main()
{
    int value;

    value = -1 - 4 + 2 * 3 - 4;

    cout << value << endl;
}
```

Problem 1.10: What is the output of the program below?

```cpp
#include <iostream>
using namespace std;

int main()
{
    int A, B = 10;

    A = 100 / (B - B*1);

    cout << A << endl;
}
```

Problem 1.11: Does the following program compile successfully?

```cpp
#include <iostream>
using namespace std;

int main()
{
    ////////////////////////////////////////////////////////////////
    ///////////////////                        /////////////
    ///////////////////                        /////////////
    ///////////////                //////////////////////////////
    ///////////////                //////////////////////////////
    ///////////////                //////////////////////////////
    ///////////////                            /////////////
    ///////////////                            /////////////
    ///////////                //////////////////////////////////
    /////////                //////////////////////////////////
    /////////                            ////////////////////
    ////////                            ////////////////////
    ////////////////////////////////////////////////////////////////
}
```

8

Problem 1.12: Does the following program compile successfully?

```cpp
#include <iostream>
using namespace std;

int main()
{
    int T = 1, E = 2, N = 3

    cout << T << E << N
}
```

Problem 1.13: Below is a program converting degrees Celsius to degrees Fahrenheit. However, the output of the program below is 52 while the correct output is 68. Please fix the program to generate the correct output.

```cpp
#include <iostream>
using namespace std;

int main()
{
    float fahrenheit;
    float celsius = 20.0;

    fahrenheit = 32.0 + celsius * ( 9 / 5 );

    cout << fahrenheit << endl;
}
```

Problem 1.14: If the following program doesn't compile, why not? If it does compile, what is the output when it is run?

```cpp
#include <iostream>
using namespace std;

int main()
{
    cout << "Please do not use" << " "
         <<                              "this coding style"
         << " " << "in" << " "              <<      "your"
         << " " << "program!!" << endl;
}
```

Problem 1.15: Does the following program compile successfully? If no, then where are the compilation errors at?

```cpp
#include <iostream>
using namespace std;

int main()
{
        // Identifiers: A C++ Identifier must start with either a letter or
        // an underscore symbol, and the remaining characters must
        // all be digits, letters, or the underscore symbol.
        // C++ identifiers are case sensitive and have no limit to their length.

        int @__#__#__@;                      // (1)

        int 987654321;                       // (2)

        int X987654321;                      // (3)

        unsigned char ten%;                  // (4)

        long double F-16;                    // (5)

        long double F16;                     // (6)

        long int t.e.n;                      // (7)

        unsigned long int ten;               // (8)

        float __;                            // (9)

        int    zzzzzzzzzzzzzzzzzzZZZZZ;      // (10)
}
```

Problem 1.16: If the following program doesn't compile, why not? If it does compile, what is the output when it is run?

```
#include <iostream>
using namespace std;

int main()
{
    cout << 0++ << endl;
}
```

Problem 1.17: What is the output of the program below?

```
#include <iostream>
using namespace std;

int main()
{
    int value = 100;

    // value++ returns the old value and then adds one to value

    cout << value++ << endl;
    cout << value     << endl;

    value = 100;

    // ++value adds one to value and then return the new value

    cout << ++value << endl;
    cout <<     value << endl;
}
```

Problem 1.18: What is the output of the program below?

```cpp
#include <iostream>
using namespace std;

int main()
{
    int value = 1;

    value -= 1;                    // same as value = value - 1;
    cout << value << endl;
    value += 1;                    // same as value = value + 1;
    cout << value << endl;

    value /= 2;                    // same as value = value / 2;
    cout << value << endl;
    value *= 2;                    // same as value = value * 2;
    cout << value << endl;
}
```

Problem 1.19: What is the output of the program below?

```cpp
#include <iostream>
using namespace std;

int main()
{
    int a=5, b = 0, c = 0;

    a /= b = 5;
    cout << a << endl;

    a = b == c;          // = and == are different in C++
    cout << a << endl;   // = is an assignment operator
                         // == is a comparison operator
    (a == b) == c;
    cout << a << endl;

    a == (b = c);
    cout << a << endl;
}
```

Problem 1.20: What is the output of the program below?

```
#include <iostream>
using namespace std;

int main()
{
    int x = 10, y = 50;
    x = y;
    y = x;                    // Does this swap the values of x and y ?

    cout << x << " " << y << endl;
}
```

Problem 1.21: What is the output of the program below?

```
#include <iostream>
using namespace std;

int main()
{
    int x = 10, y = 50, z;
    z = x;
    x = y;
    y = z;                    // Does this swap the values of x and y ?

    cout << x << " " << y << endl;
}
```

Problem 1.22: What is the output of the program below?

```
#include <iostream>
using namespace std;

int main()
{
    int x = 10, y = 50;
    x = x + y;
    y = x - y;
    x = x - y;                // Does this swap the values of x and y ?

    cout << x << " " << y << endl;
}
```

Practice 1 – Solution

1.1: Compilation error because variable names are case-sensitive.

1.2: Compilation error because `double` is a reserved keyword.

1.3: Compilation error because `float` is a reserved keyword.

1.4:
```cpp
#include <iostream>
using namespace std;

int main()
{
    cout << "C++";
}
```

1.5:
```cpp
#include <iostream>
using namespace std;

int main()
{
    int x;

    cin >> x;

    cout << x + 100 << endl;
}
```

1.6:
```cpp
#include <iostream>
using namespace std;

int main()
{
    int X, A, B, C, D, E;

    cin >> X ;

    A = 4 * X;

    B = A / 100;

    C = A - B;

    D = A + 2 * B + 3 * C;

    E = A + B + C + D + X;

    cout << A << endl << B << endl << C << endl;
    cout << D << endl << E << endl;
}
```

1.7: 40

1.8: 0 because integer division makes 19/20 as 0.

1.9: -3

1.10: The program will crash at execution time because of division by zero error.

1.11: This program does compile successfully and output nothing to the console as comments are omitted by C++ compilers.

1.12: Compilation error because of missing semicolons.

1.13: This program can be fixed by changing 9 to 9.0 or 5 to 5.0 or both to avoid doing integer division.

1.14: The output is:

Please do not use this coding style in your program!!

1.15: (1)(2)(4)(5)(7) are invalid C++ identifiers.

1.16: Compilation error because ++ operator cannot be applied to a constant.

1.17: 100

101

101

101

1.18: 0

1

0

0

1.19: 1

0   *A false comparison result is translated as integer 0.

0

0

1.20: 50 50   *The codes do not swap the values of x and y

1.21: 50 10   *The codes swap the values of x and y

1.22: 50 10   *The codes swap the values of x and y

Practice 2 – If-else

```cpp
#include <iostream>
using namespace std;

int main()
{
    int x = 100, y = 100;
    if (x <= y)
        cout << "x is lesser than or equal to y." << endl;
    else
        cout << "x is greater than y." << endl;
}
```

```cpp
#include <iostream>
using namespace std;

int main()
{
    if (-614)
        cout << "Minus number is evaluated as true!" << endl;
    else
        cout << "Minus number is evaluated as false!" << endl;
}
```

```cpp
#include <iostream>
using namespace std;

int main()
{
    int x = 50, y = 100;

    if (x = y)      // be careful with = and ==
        cout << "x and y are equal!" << endl;
    else
        cout << "x and y are NOT equal!" << endl;
}
```

```cpp
#include <iostream>
using namespace std;

int main()
{
    int x = 100.49999999999999999999;

    cout << x << endl;

    if (x==100)
        cout << "Right! ";
            cout << "x = 100!" << endl;

    cout << "No compilation error?" << endl;
}
```

```cpp
#include <iostream>
using namespace std;

int main()
{
    int x = 100.49999999999999999999;

    if(x==100)
        cout << "Right! ";
        cout << "x = 100!" << endl;
    else
        cout << "No! ";
        cout << "x = 101!" << endl;
}
```

Problem 2.6: What is the output of the program below?

```cpp
#include <iostream>
using namespace std;

int main()
{
    int a=1,b=2;

    if (a==b) ;                          // Extra semicolon here
    {
        cout << "a equals to b" << endl;
    }
    if (a!=b) ;
    {
        cout << "a is not equal to b" << endl;
    }
}
```

Problem 2.7: What is the output of the program below?

```cpp
#include <iostream>
using namespace std;

int main()
{
    int a=1, b= -1000;

    if ( b > 0) if (b < 0) a = 2;
    else b = 3;

    cout << "a = " << a << endl;
}
```

Problem 2.8: What is the output of the program below?

```cpp
#include <iostream>
using namespace std;

int main()
{
    int x=0,y=9;

    if (( x == 0 ) && ( y < 20 ))
        cout << "1";
    if (( y > 20 ) || ( x <   5 ))
        cout << "2" << endl;
    if ( x == 12 )
        cout << "4" << endl;
    if (( x == 1) && ( 32767+x < 3641*y ))
        cout << "5" << endl;
}
```

Problem 2.9: What is the output of the program below?

```cpp
#include <iostream>
using namespace std;

int main()
{
    int x = 100;

    if (x <   6666)
    if (x <   5555)
    if (x <   4444)
    if (x <   2222)
        cout << "x < 2222" << endl;
    else
        cout << "x = 100" << endl;
}
```

Problem 2.10: Please write a multiway if-else statement to print appropriate messages based on the value of an integer variable when n < 10 or 10 <= n <= 50 or n > 50

```cpp
#include <iostream>
using namespace std;

int main()
{
    int n;
    cin >> n;

    if (                                        )
        cout << "n less than 10 " << endl;

    else if (                                   )
        cout << "10 <= n <= 50 " << endl;

    else if (                                   )
        cout << "n > 50 " << endl;
}
```

Problem 2.11: What is the output of the program below?

```cpp
#include <iostream>
using namespace std;

int main()
{
    if ( 1 <= 2 <= 3 )                 // bad coding style! Don't do this!!
        cout << "does this work?" << endl;
}
```

Problem 2.12: What is the output of the program below?

```cpp
#include <iostream>
using namespace std;

int main()
{
    if ( 1 <= 2 && 2 <= 3 )
        cout << "does this also work?" << endl;
}
```

Problem 2.13: What is the output of the program below if the input is abc?

```
#include <iostream>
#include <string>
using namespace std;

int main()
{
    string str;
    cin >> str;
    if(str == "abc")
        cout << "YES" << endl;
    else
        cout << "NO" << endl;
}
```

Problem 2.14: If the following program doesn't compile, why not? If it does compile, what is the output when it is run?

```
#include <iostream>
#include <string>
using namespace std;

int main()
{
    const string str = "Hello World!";

    cout << str << endl;

    if(str == "Hello World!")
        str = "CS31";

    cout << str << endl;
}
```

Practice 2 – Solution

2.1:   x is lesser than or equal to y.

2.2:   Minus number is evaluated as true!

2.3:   x and y are equal!

2.4:   100

Right! x = 100!

No compilation error?

2.5:   Compilation error. This program should be fixed by using { }

2.6:   a equals to b

a is not equal to b

2.7:   a = 1

2.8:   12

2.9:   x < 2222

2.10:
```
#include <iostream>
using namespace std;

int main()
{
    int n;
    cin >> n;

    if ( n < 10)
        cout << "n less than 10 " << endl;

    else if ( 10 <= n && n <= 50)
        cout << "10 <= n <= 50 " << endl;

    else if ( n > 50)
        cout << "n > 50 " << endl;
}
```

2.11:   Does this work?

2.12:   Does this also work?

2.13:   YES

2.14:   Compilation error because a constant string variable cannot be re-assigned another value.

Practice 3 – Loop

Problem 3.1: What is the output of the program below?

```cpp
#include <iostream>
using namespace std;

int main()
{
    // for( initialization; stay-in-loop-condition; prepare-for-next-iteration)
    // { statements; }
    // initialization -> check stay-in-loop-condition -> prepare for-next-
    // iteration -> check stay-in-loop-condition ->...
    int i;

    for(i = 0; i <= 0; i++)
        cout << "Hello Loop!" << endl;

    cout << "i = " << i << endl;
}
```

Problem 3.2: What is the output of the program below?

```cpp
#include <iostream>
using namespace std;

int main()
{
    // For Loop syntax:
    // for( initialization; stay-in-loop-condition; prepare-for-next-iteration)
    // { statements; }
    int i;

    for(i = 0; i < 0; i++)
        cout << "Hello Loop!" <<   endl;

    cout << "i = " << i << endl;
}
```

Problem 3.3: What is the output of the program below?

```cpp
#include <iostream>
using namespace std;

int main()
{
    // For Loop syntax:
    // for( initialization; stay-in-loop-condition; prepare-for-next-iteration)
    // { statements; }
    int i;

    for(i = 0; i < 1; i++)
        cout << "Hello Loop!" << endl;

    cout << "i = " << i << endl;
}
```

Problem 3.4: What is the output of the program below?

```cpp
#include <iostream>
using namespace std;

int main()
{
    int a=2,b=1;

    for(int i=0;i<4;i++)
        b = b*a;

    cout << b << endl;
}
```

Problem 3.5: What is the output of the program below?

```cpp
#include <iostream>
using namespace std;

int main()
{
    int a=2,b=1;

    for(int i=0;i<=4;i++)
        b = b*a;

    cout << b << endl;
}
```

Problem 3.6: If the following program doesn't compile, why not? If it does compile, what is the output when it is run?

```cpp
#include <iostream>
using namespace std;

int main()
{
    int a=2,b=1;

    for(int i=0;i<=4;i++);   // There is a semicolon here
        b = b*a;

    cout << b << endl;
}
```

Problem 3.7: If the following program doesn't compile, why not? If it does compile, what is the output when it is run?

```cpp
#include <iostream>
using namespace std;

int main()
{
    for(              ;              ;              )
                          ;


}
```

Problem 3.8: What is the output of the program below?

```cpp
#include <iostream>
using namespace std;

int main()
{
    int x;

    // We want to find the solution for
    // x^2 - 8x + 15 = 0

    for(x=0; x<=5; x++)
        if ( (x*x - 8*x + 15) == 0 )
            cout << "x = " << x << endl;
}
```

Problem 3.9: What is the output of the program below?

```cpp
#include <iostream>
using namespace std;

int main()
{
    int x=0,count=0; // Initialization

    // While Syntax:
    // while(stay-in-loop-condition is true)
    // {              statements;              }

    while(count != 2) // stay-in-loop-condition
    {
        if ( (x*x - 8*x + 15) == 0 )
        {
            cout << "x = " << x << endl;
            count++;   // prepare-for-next-iteration
        }
        x++;
    }
}
```

```cpp
#include <iostream>
using namespace std;
int main()
{
    for(int i=0, double j = 100 ; i < 10 ; i++ , j++ )
                    ;

    cout << "i = " << i << ", j = " << j << endl;
}
```

```cpp
#include <iostream>
using namespace std;
int main()
{
    int i;

    for(i=0;i<3;i++)
        cout << i << endl;
        cout << i << endl;
}
```

```cpp
#include <iostream>
using namespace std;
int main()
{
    int i   =                                    ;

    while (                                            )
    {
        cout << i << endl;
        i++;
    }

    cout << i << endl;
}
```

Problem 3.13: What is the output of the program below?
```
#include <iostream>
using namespace std;

int main()
{
    int i=0;
    double j=100;

    for(; i < 10 ; i++ , j++ )
            ;
    cout << "i = " << i << ", j = " << j << endl;
}
```

Problem 3.14: What is the output of the program below?
```
#include <iostream>
using namespace std;

int main()
{
    int i;
    double j;

    for( i = 0 , j = 100 ; (i < 10) && (j < 110) ; i++ , j++ )
            ;

    cout << "i = " << i << ", j = " << j << endl;
}
```

Problem 3.15: What is the output of the program below?

```cpp
#include <iostream>
using namespace std;

int main()
{
    int i , j;

    for( i = 0 ; i < 2 ; i++ )
        for( j = 0 ; j < 2 ; j++ )
            cout << i * j;
            cout << endl;
}
```

Problem 3.16: What is the output of the program below?

```cpp
#include <iostream>
using namespace std;

int main()
{
    int i, j, k;

    for( i = 0 ; i < 2 ; i++ )
        for( j = 0 ; j < 2 ; j++ )
            for( k = 0 ; k < 2 ; k++ )
                cout << i * j * k ;
                cout << endl;
}
```

Problem 3.17: What is the output of the program below?

```cpp
#include <iostream>
using namespace std;

int main()
{
    int n = 0, a = 2, b = 1;

    while(n!=4)
    {
        b = b*a;
        n++;
    }

    cout << a << " to the power of " << n << "   =   " << b << endl;
}
```

Problem 3.18: What is the output of the program below?

```cpp
#include <iostream>
using namespace std;

int main()
{
    int n=4,a=2,b=1;

    while(n != 0)
    {
        b = b*a;
        n--;
    }

    // Is the output the same as the output from problem 3.17 ?
    cout << a << " to the power of " << n << "   =   " << b << endl;
}
```

Problem 3.19: What is the output of the program below?

```cpp
#include <iostream>
using namespace std;

int main()
{
    int n=4,a=2,b=1;

    while(n!=4)
    {
        b = b*a;
        n++;
    }

    cout << a << " to the power of " << n << "   =   " << b << endl;
}
```

Problem 3.20: Convert the program from Problem 3.19 by using a for loop

```cpp
#include <iostream>
using namespace std;

int main()
{
    int n=4,a=2,b=1;

    for (                                    )
        b = b*a;

    cout << b << endl;

}
```

Problem 3.21: If the following program doesn't compile, why not? If it does compile, what is the output when it is run?

```cpp
#include <iostream>
using namespace std;

int main()
{
    int a = 1;      // Syntax for do-while
                    // do the statement at least once and then test the condition
                    // If condition is false, exit. If true, then loop.
                    // But in this program, something is wrong…
    do
    {
        a = 2;
    } while (1 !=0)

    cout << "a = " << a << endl;
}
```

Problem 3.22: What is the output of the program below?

```cpp
#include <iostream>
using namespace std;

int main()
{
    int a = 1;

    do
    {
        a = 2;
    } while (1 !=0);     // This time there's something wrong again…

    cout << "a = " << a << endl;
}
```

Problem 3.23: What is the output of the program below?

```cpp
#include <iostream>
using namespace std;

int main()
{
    int a = 1;

    do
    {
        a = 2;
    } while (1!=1);

    cout << "a = " << a << endl;
}
```

Problem 3.24: What is the output of the program below?

```cpp
#include <iostream>
using namespace std;

int main()
{
    int a = 0;

    while ( a < 5) a++;

    cout << "a = " << a << endl;
}
```

Problem 3.25: What is the output of the program below?

```cpp
#include <iostream>
using namespace std;

int main()
{
    int x = 2, y = 3, z = 0, n = 0;

    while ( n != y )
    {
        n = n + 1;
        z = z + x;
    }

    if ( z == (x * y) )
        cout << "z = x times y." << endl;
    else
        cout << "Trap!!" << endl;
}
```

Problem 3.26: What is the output of the program below?

```cpp
#include <iostream>
using namespace std;

int main()
{
    int x = -100;

    do
    {
        cout << x << endl;
        x = x - 5;
    } while(x > 0);
}
```

Problem 3.27: What is the output of the program below?

```cpp
#include <iostream>
using namespace std;

int main()
{
    int i;

    for(i = 1 ; i < 10 ; i += 2 )
        cout << i << endl;
}
```

Problem 3.28: Please re-write the program from problem 3.27 by using do-while loop.

```cpp
#include <iostream>
using namespace std;

int main()
{
    int i = _____ // Fill in the blanks

    do
    {

        cout << i << endl;


        _____

    } while( _____ );

}
```

Problem 3.29: What is the output of the program below?

```cpp
#include<iostream>
using namespace std;

int main()
{
    for(int month = 1;month<=2; month++ )
    {
        switch(month)
        {
            case 1: cout << "January has 31 days" << endl;
                    break;
            case 12: cout << "December has 31 days" << endl;
                    break;
            default: cout << "?" << endl; break;
        }
    }
}
```

Problem 3.30: What is the output of the program below?

```cpp
#include<iostream>
using namespace std;

int main()
{
    for(int month = 1;month<=3; month++ )
    {
        switch(month)
        {
            case '1': cout << "January has 31 days" << endl;
            case '3': cout << "March has 31 days" << endl;
            default: cout << "?" << endl;
        }
    }
}
// Is case '1' the same as case 1 ?
```

Problem 3.31: What is the output of the program below?

```cpp
#include <iostream>
#include <string>
using namespace std;

int main()
{
    int numOfChars = 0, numOfDigits = 0;
    int numOfUpperChars = 0, numOfLowerChars = 0;

    string s = "It is a beautiful day!";

    s[0] = tolower(s[0]);
    s[6] = toupper(s[6]);

    for(int i = 0 ; i != s.size() ; i++)
    {
        if(isalpha(s[i])) numOfChars++;

        if(isdigit(s[i])) numOfDigits++;

        if(islower(s[i])) numOfLowerChars++;

        if(isupper(s[i])) numOfUpperChars++;
    }

    cout << numOfChars << " " << numOfDigits << endl;
    cout << numOfUpperChars << " " << numOfLowerChars << endl;

}
```

Practice 3 – Solution

3.1:   Hello Loop!
            i = 1

3.2:   i = 0

3.3:   Hello Loop!
            i = 1

3.4:   16

3.5:   32

3.6:   No compilation error. The output is 2

3.7:   No compilation error. This is an infinite loop.

3.8:   x = 3
            x = 5

3.9:   x = 3
            x = 5

3.10:   Compilation error because the lifespan of variables i,j only exist inside the for-loop.

3.11:   0
            1
            2
            3

3.12:

```cpp
#include <iostream>
using namespace std;
int main()
{
    int i = 0;

    while ( i < 3 )
    {
        cout << i << endl;
        i++;
    }

    cout << i << endl;
}
```

3.13:   i = 10, j = 110

3.14:   i = 10, j = 110

3.15:   0001

3.16:   00000001

3.17:   2 to the power of 4   = 16

3.18:   2 to the power of 0   = 16

3.19:   2 to the power of 4   = 1

3.20:
```
#include <iostream>
using namespace std;

int main()
{
    int n = 4, a = 2, b = 1;

    for ( ; n != 4 ; n++ )
        b = b*a;

    cout << b << endl;
}
```

3.21: Compilation error because of missing semicolon.

3.22: Infinite loop.

3.23: $a = 2$

3.24: $a = 5$

3.25: $z = x$ times y.

3.26: -100

3.27:
1

3

5

7

9

3.28:
```
#include <iostream>
using namespace std;

int main()
{
    int i = 1;

    do
    {
        cout << i << endl;
        i += 2;
    } while( i < 10 );
}
```

3.29: January has 31 days

?

3.30: ?

?

?

1 is integer 1. But '1' is integer 49 because '1' is the 50th encoded character in ASCII endcoding. Check http://www.asciitable.com/ for more details

3.31: 17 0

1 16

Practice Midterm 1

Problem	Maximal Possible Points	Received
1	3	
2	5	
3	3	
4	3	
5	3	
6	3	
7	7	
8	5	
Total Score	32	

Problem #1: What is the output of the program below?

```cpp
#include <iostream>
#include <string>
#include <cctype>
using namespace std;

int main()
{
    const string str = "There is an Apple!";
        int count=0;

    for(int i=0 ; i != str.size() ; i++)
        if( str[i] == 'a' && isalpha(str[i]) )
            count++;

    cout << count << endl;
}
```

(1) 1
(2) 2
(3) 3
(4) 4
(5) 5
(6) No output. There is a Compilation Error.

Problem #2: Which of the following code segments produce the exact output as the sample program provided below? Suppose each choice uses the same header files (#include...). There may be more than one answer.

```cpp
#include <iostream>
#include <string>
using namespace std;

int main()
{
    for(int i=0;i<2;i++) {
        for(int j=0;j<=i;j++)
            cout << "*" ;
        cout << endl;
    }
}
```

(1)
```cpp
int main()
{
    for(int i = 2 ; i >= 1 ; i-- ) {
        for(int j = 0 ; j <= i ; j++ )
            cout << "*" ;
        cout << endl;
    }
}
```

(2)
```cpp
int main()
{
    for(int i = 2 ; i >= 1 ; i-- ) {
        for(int j = 0 ; j < i ; j++ )
            cout << "*" ;
        cout << endl;
    }
}
```

(3)
```cpp
int main()
{
    for(int i = 2 ; i >= 1 ; i-- ) {
        for(int j = 3 ; j > i ; j-- )
            cout << "*" ;
        cout << endl;
    }
}
```

(4)
```cpp
int main()
{
    for(int i = 2 ; i >= 1 ; i-- ) {
        for(int j = 2 ; j >= i ; j-- )
            cout << "*" ;
        cout << endl;
    }
}
```

(5)
```cpp
int main()
{
    for(int i = 2 ; i >= 1 ; i-- ) {
        for(int j = i+1 ; j >= i ; j-- )
            cout << "*" ;
        cout << endl;
    }
}
```

(6)
```cpp
int main()
{
    for(int i = 5 ; i >= 4 ; i-- ) {
        for(int j = 5 ; j >= i ; j-- )
            cout << "*" ;
        cout << endl;
    }
}
```

```cpp
#include <iostream>
#include <string>
using namespace std;

int main()
{
    string str = "abcdefga";
    int value = 0;

    for(int i = 0 ; i != str.size() ; i++ ) {
        for(int j = i + 1 ; j != str.size() ; j++ ) {
            if( str[ i ] == str[ j ] ) {
                value = j - i;
            }
        }
    }

    cout << value << endl;
}
```

(1) 1
(2) 2
(3) 3
(4) 4
(5) 5
(6) 6
(7) 7
(8) 8
(9) 9
(10) 10
(11) 11
(12) 12
(13) No output. There is a Compilation Error.

```cpp
#include <iostream>
#include <string>
using namespace std;

int main()
{
    int i = 0,value = 0;

    for( i = 0 ; i < 5 ; i++ ){
        switch( i ) {
        case 1: value = i + 1;
        case 2: value = value - 1;
        case 3: value = value + 1;
        case 4: value = value + 2; break;
        case 5: value = value - 1;
        default: value = value + 1;
        }
    }

    cout << value << endl;
}
```

(1) 1
(2) 2
(3) 3
(4) 4
(5) 5
(6) 6
(7) 7
(8) 8
(9) 9
(10) 10
(11) 11
(12) 12
(13) 13
(14) 14
(15) No output. There is Compilation Error

Problem #5: What is the output of the program below?

```cpp
#include <iostream>
#include <string>
using namespace std;

int main()
{
    int i = 0;

    do {
        for(int j = i ; j >= 0 ; j-- )
            cout << "*" ;
        cout << endl;
        i++;
    } while(i<4);
}
```

(1)
*
**
***
****
(2)
*
**
***
(3)
***
**
*
(4)
****
***
**
*

Problem #6: What is the output of the program below?

```cpp
#include <iostream>
#include <string>
using namespace std;

int main()
{
    string exp = "-3+3+555+99999";

    int mult = 1;
    int offs = 0;
    for(int i=0;i != exp.size() ; i += 2) {
        if( exp[ i ] == '-' )
            mult = i+5;
        else if( exp[ i ] == '+' )
            mult = i+8;
        else
            offs = 1;
    }
    cout << exp[offs] << exp[mult % exp.size() ] << endl;
}
```

(1) 5+
(2) 99
(3) -3
(4) 3+
(5) 33
(6) 55
(7) 5+
(8) +5
(9) 35
(10) 53
(11) 59
(12) 39
(13) 93
(14) -9
(15) 9+

Problem #7: Please use switch-case to write a program below to output a student's grade based on the following conditions:
If a student's grade is from 90 to 100, then it's A (just cout << "A" << endl;)
If a student's grade is less than 90, but greater than or equal to 80, then it's B.
If a student's grade is less than 80, but greater than or equal to 70, then it's C.
If a student's grade is less than 70, but greater than or equal to 60, then it's D.
Otherwise, it's F.
If you do not use switch-case to write your program, you'll get zero points.
You can only use 1 extra variable. Failure to comply gets zero points.

```cpp
#include <iostream>
using namespace std;

int main() {
        int score = 0;
        cout << "Please enter the student's score:";
        cin >> score;




}
```

Problem #8: Please write a do-while loop to find the first lower case character in a given string. If there is no lower case letter, the program outputs "No lowercase character". If there is a lower case character, output the first lower case character. If your program gets stuck in an infinite loop, you'll get zero points.

```cpp
#include <iostream>
#include <cctype>
#include <string>
using namespace std;

int main() {
    int i;

    string str;

    cin >> str;




    if (                                              )
        cout << "No lowercase character" << endl;
    else
        cout << str[i] << endl;
}
```

Practice Midterm 1 – Solution

1: (1)
2: (3)(4)(6)
3: (7)
4: (11)
5: (1)
6: (4)
7:
```cpp
#include <iostream>
using namespace std;

int main() {
    int score = 0;

    cout << "Please enter the student's score:";
    cin >> score;

    int choice = score / 10;

    switch (choice) {
    case 10:
    case 9:
        cout << "A" << endl;
        break;
    case 8:
        cout << "B" << endl;
        break;
    case 7:
        cout << "C" << endl;
        break;
    case 6:
        cout << "D" << endl;
        break;
    default:
        cout << "F" << endl;
    }
}
```
8:
```cpp
#include <iostream>
#include <cctype>
#include <string>
using namespace std;

int main() {
    int i;
    string str;
    cin >> str;
    i = -1;
    do {
        i++;
    } while (i != str.size() && !islower(str[i]));

    if (i == str.size())
        cout << "No lowercase character" << endl;
    else
        cout << str[i] << endl;
}
```

Practice 4 –Function and String

Problem 4.1: What is the output of the program below?

```
#include <iostream>
using namespace std;

int main()
{
    // We want to find the solutions to x^2 - 8x + 15
    // Solutions are:

    for(int x=0;x<=10;x++)
        if( (x*x - 8*x + 15) == 0)
            cout << "x = " << x << " ";
    cout << endl;
}
```

Problem 4.2: What is the output of the program below?

```
#include <iostream>
using namespace std;

int find_solutions(int x)
{
    return (x*x - 8*x + 15);
}

int main()
{
    // We want to find the solutions to x^2 - 8x + 15
    // Solutions are:

    for(int x=0;x<=10;x++)
        if( find_solutions(x) == 0)
            cout << "x = " << x << " ";
    cout << endl;
}
```

Problem 4.3: What is the output of the program below?

```cpp
#include <iostream>
using namespace std;

void find_solutions(int x)
{
    if( (x*x - 8*x + 15) == 0)
        cout << "x = " << x << " ";
}

int main()
{
    // We want to find the solutions to x^2 - 8x + 15
    // Solutions are:

    for(int x=0;x<=10;x++)
        find_solutions(x);
    cout << endl;
}
```

Problem 4.4: What is the output of the program below?

```cpp
#include <iostream>
using namespace std;

// Compute the area of a triangle
double area(double L,double H)
{
    return (L * H / 2.0);
}

int main()
{
    double a = area(10.0, 5.0);

    cout << "Area = " << a << endl;
}
```

Problem 4.5: Please complete the function definition, mysteriousFunction , to compute x to the power of (y + 3) by using pow() function.

```cpp
#include <iostream>
#include <cmath>
using namespace std;

double mysteriousFunction(double x,double y)
{

}
int main()
{
    double x = 10, y = 1, z;

    z = mysteriousFunction(x, y);

    cout << x << " to the power of " << y+3 << " is: " << z << endl;
}
```

Problem 4.6: Please complete the function definition to compute x to the power of square root of (x + y) by using sqrt() and pow() functions.

```cpp
#include <iostream>
#include <cmath>
using namespace std;

double mysteriousFunction (double x,double y)
{

}
int main()
{
    double x = 2, y = 2, z;

    z = mysteriousFunction (x,y);

    cout << x << " to the power of " <<                      << " is: "
        << z << endl;
}
```

Problem 4.7: Please define a function to compute $\dfrac{-b \pm \sqrt{b^2 - 4ac}}{2a}$

```cpp
#include <iostream>
#include <cmath>
using namespace std;

void computeRoots(double a, double b, double c)
{
    double d = _____

    double e = _____

    cout << d << endl << e << endl;
}
int main()
{
    // Compute the roots for x² - 5x + 4 = 0

    double a = 1,b = -5,c = 4;

    computeRoots(a, b, c);
}
```

Problem 4.8: If the following program doesn't compile, why not? If it does compile, what is the output when it is run?

```cpp
#include <iostream>
using namespace std;
int sum(int n1, int n2, int n3)
{
    int sum2(int n4, int n5, int n6)
    { return (n4 + n5 + n6); }
    return (n1 + n2 + n3 + sum2(n1, n2, n3));
}
int main()
{
    int x = 1, y = 2, z = 3;
    cout << sum( x, y, z) << endl;
}
```

```
#include <iostream>
using namespace std;

int sum2(int,int,int);

int sum(int n1, int n2, int n3)
{
    return (n1 + n2 + n3 + sum2(n1, n2, n3));
}
int main()
{
    int sum2(int n4, int n5, int n6)
    { return (n4 + n5 + n6); }

    int x = 1, y = 2, z = 3;
    cout << sum( x, y, z) << endl;
}
```

```
#include <iostream>
using namespace std;

int main()
{
    bool found = false;

    string str = "123456";

    for(int i=0;i != str.size() ; i++)
        if( str[i] == '3' )
            found = true;

    if(found)
        cout << "We found 3!!" << endl;
}
```

Problem 4.11: Please write a function called integerDivision. The requirement is that if y is ZERO, then output "Cannot divide by zero" and do nothing (return back to main function). Otherwise, output the value of x divide by y.

```cpp
#include <iostream>
using namespace std;

// Implement integerDivision function here.




int main()
{
    int x, y;

    cin >> x >> y ;

    integerDivision(x, y);
}
```

Problem 4.12: What is the output of the program below?

```cpp
#include <iostream>
using namespace std;

int main()
{
    int x = 1, y = 0;
    integerDivision(x, y);
}

void integerDivision(int x, int y)
{
    if(y == 0)
    {
        cout << "Cannot divide by ZERO!" << endl;
        return ;
    }
    cout << x/y << endl;
}
```

Problem 4.13: What is the output of the program below?

```cpp
#include <iostream>
using namespace std;

// Pass by value
void changeXandY(int a, int b)
{
    a = 5; b = 5;
}

int main()
{
    int x = 1, y = 1;

    changeXandY(x, y);

    cout << x << endl << y << endl;
}
```

Problem 4.14: What is the output of the program below?

```cpp
#include <iostream>
using namespace std;

// pass by reference
void changeXandY(int &a, int &b)
{
    a = 5; b = 5;
}

int main()
{
    int x = 1, y = 1;
    changeXandY(x, y);
    cout << x << endl << y << endl;
}
```

Problem 4.15: What is the output of the program below?

```cpp
#include <iostream>
using namespace std;

int main()
{
    int x = 10;
    cout << x << endl;
    {
        cout << x << endl;
        int x = 100;
        cout << x << endl;
        x = 200;
    }
    cout << x << endl;
}
```

```
#include <iostream>
using namespace std;

void changeXandY(int &a, int &b)
{
    a = 5; b = 5;
}

int main()
{
    changeXandY(int x=1, int y=1);
    cout << x << endl << y << endl;
}
```

```
#include <iostream>
#include <string>
using namespace std;

int countNonChar(string s)
{
    int total = 0;
    for (int k = 0; k != s.size(); k++)
    {
        if ( !isalpha(s[k]) )
            total++;
    }
    return total;
}

int main()
{
    string str = "Hello World!";
    cout << countNonChar(str) << endl;
}
```

Problem 4.18: If the following program doesn't compile, why not? If it does compile, what is the output when it is run?

```cpp
#include <iostream>
#include <string>
using namespace std;
int countNonChar(string s)
{
    int total = 0;
    for (int k = 0; k != s.size(); k++)
    {
        if (!isalpha(s[k]))
            total++;
    }
    return total;
}
int main()
{
    char ch = 'C';
    cout << countNonChar(ch) << endl;
    // Does countNonChar("C") work?
}
```

Problem 4.19: What is the output of the program below?

```cpp
#include <iostream>
#include <string>
using namespace std;

bool containsTwoChars(string s, string sub1)
{
    for (int k = 0; k != s.size()-1; k++)
    {
        if ((s[k] == sub1[0]) && (s[k+1] == sub1[1]) ) return true;
    }
    return false;
}
int main()
{
    if (containsTwoChars("Computer Science 31", "31"))
        cout << "Learning C++ is not as easy as it seems!" << endl;
}
```

Problem 4.20: What is the output of the program below?

```cpp
#include <iostream>
#include <string>
using namespace std;

int main()
{
    string result="";
    result = result + "Hello ";
    result += "World!";
    cout << result << endl;
}
```

Problem 4.21: What is the output of the program below?

```cpp
#include <iostream>
#include <string>
using namespace std;

int main()
{
    string str = "HELLO WORLD!";

    cout << "length of str is: " << str.size() << endl;

    string result;

    for (size_t k = 0; k != str.size(); k++)
        result += tolower(str[k]);
    cout << result << endl;
}
```

```cpp
#include <iostream>
#include <string>
using namespace std;

int main()
{
    string str = "HELLO WORLD!";
    string result;

    for (size_t k = 0; k != str.size(); k++)
        result += tolower(str[k]);

    cout << result << endl;

    cout << result.substr(0,5) << endl;
    cout << result.substr(6,6) << endl;
}
```

```cpp
#include<iostream>
using namespace std;

void output(int p, int q)
{
    cout << "Integer output!\n";
}

void output(double p, double q)
{
    cout << "Double output!\n";
}

int main()
{
    int x = 1, y = 1;
    double a = 1.0, b = 1.0;
    output(x,y);
    output(a,b);
}
```

Problem 4.24: If the following program doesn't compile, why not? If it does compile, what is the output when it is run?

```cpp
#include<iostream>
using namespace std;

void output(int p, int q)
{
    cout << "Integer output!\n";
}

void output(double p, double q)
{
    cout << "Double output!\n";
}

int main()
{
    int x = 1, y = 1;
    double a = 1.0, b = 1.0;
    output(x,y);
    output(a,b);
    output(x,b);
}
```

Problem 4.25: What is the output of the program below?

```cpp
#include<iostream>
using namespace std;

void output(int p, int q=1)
{
    cout << "p = " << p << " q = " << q << endl;
}

int main()
{
    int x = 10, y = 10;
    output(x);
    output(x,y);
}
```

Practice 4 – Solution

4.1:   x = 3 x = 5
4.2:   x = 3 x = 5
4.3:   x = 3 x = 5
4.4:   Area = 25
4.5:

```cpp
#include <iostream>
#include <cmath>
using namespace std;

double mysteriousFunction(double x, double y)
{
    return pow(x, y + 3);
}
int main()
{
    double x = 10, y = 1, z;

    z = mysteriousFunction(x, y);

    cout << x << " to the power of " << y + 3 << " is: " << z << endl;
}
```

4.6:

```cpp
#include <iostream>
#include <cmath>
using namespace std;

double mysteriousFunction(double x, double y)
{
    return pow(x, sqrt(x + y));
}
int main()
{
    double x = 2, y = 2, z;

    z = mysteriousFunction(x, y);

    cout << x << " to the power of " << sqrt(x+y) << " is: "
        << z << endl;
}
```

4.7:

```cpp
#include <iostream>
#include <cmath>
using namespace std;
void computeRoots(double a, double b, double c)
{
    double d = (-b + sqrt(b*b - 4 * a*c)) / (2 * a);

    double e = (-b - sqrt(b*b - 4 * a*c)) / (2 * a);

    cout << d << endl << e << endl;
}
int main()
{
    // Compute the roots for x^2-5x+4 = 0
    double a = 1, b = -5, c = 4;
    computeRoots(a, b, c);
}
```

4.8: Compilation error because C++ does not support nested functions (define a function inside another function).

4.9: Still compilation error because C++ does not support nested functions (main is also a function).

4.10: We found 3!!

4.11:
```cpp
#include <iostream>
using namespace std;

// Implement integerDivision function here.
void integerDivision(int x, int y)
{
    if (y == 0)
    {
        cout << "Cannot divide by ZERO!" << endl;
        return;
    }
    cout << x / y << endl;
}

int main()
{
    int x, y;

    cin >> x >> y;

    integerDivision(x, y);
}
```

4.12: integerDivision function needs to be declared first before being used.

4.13: 1
1

4.14: 5
5

4.15: 10
10
100
10

4.16: Compilation error because a variable cannot be declared inside the function arguments.

4.17: 2

4.18: Compilation error because any one of the string's overloaded constructors do not take a single char as argument. Use string ch = "C" instead of char ch = 'C' here.

4.19: Learning C++ is not as easy as it seems!

4.20: Hello World!

4.21: length of str is: 12
hello world!

4.22: hello world!
hello
world!

4.23: Integer output!
Double output!

4.24: Compilation error because both overloaded functions can be used for output(x,b) and the compiler does not know which one to use.

4.25: p = 10 q = 1
p = 10 q = 10

Practice 5 – ASCII, String, and Array

Problem 5.1: What is the output of the program below?

```cpp
#include <iostream>
using namespace std;

int main()
{
    char ch = '0';              // Suppose the code number for '0' is x
    ch++;                       // now ch is '1' (x+1)

    cout << ch << endl;
    cout << (int)ch << endl;    // force ch to be integer type

    ch += 7;                    // now ch is '8' (since (x+1)+7 is x+8)

    cout << ch << endl;
    cout << (int)ch << endl;    // force ch to be integer type

    int n = ch;                 // n is the code number for '8' (i.e., x+8)

    cout << n << endl;
    cout << (char)n << endl;    // force integer n to be char type

    int m = ch - '3';           //    '8' - '3'
                                //    = (x+8) - (x+3)
                                //    = 8 - 3
                                //    so m is 5
    cout << m << endl;
}
```

```
#include <iostream>
#include <string>
using namespace std;

int convertStringToInteger(string str)
{
    int i,num=0;
    for(i=0;i != str.size() ; i++)
    {
        num = num*10 + str[i];
    }
    return num;
}

int main()
{
    string nstr = "375";
    int number = convertStringToInteger(nstr);
    cout << number << endl;
}
```

```
#include <iostream>
#include <string>
using namespace std;

int main()
{
    string str="10R3LSH12L5RSB3RSF";
    int index;

    for(index = 1; index != str.size() ; index++ )
        str[index]++;

    cout << str[index] << endl;
}
```

Problem 5.4: What is the output of the program below?

```cpp
#include <iostream>
using namespace std;

int main()
{
    int x[5] = {1,2,3,4,5};
    int sum = 0;

    for(int i = 0 ; i < 5 ; i++)
        sum += x[ i ];

    cout << "sum of 1 to 5 is: " << sum << endl;
}
```

Problem 5.5: If the following program doesn't compile, why not? If it does compile, what is the output when it is run?

```cpp
#include <iostream>
using namespace std;

int main()
{
    int x[ 4 ] = {1,2,3,4,5};
    int sum = 0;

    for(int i = 0 ; i < 5 ; i++)
        sum += x[ i ];

    cout << "sum of 1 to 5 is: " << sum << endl;
}
```

Problem 5.6: What is the output of the program below?

```cpp
#include <iostream>
using namespace std;

int main()
{
    int x[    ] = {1,2,3,4,5};  // [] makes C++ compiler figure out the size
                                // of the array.
    int sum = 0;

    for(int i = 0 ; i < 5 ; i++)
        sum += x[ i ];

    cout << "sum of 1 to 5 is: " << sum << endl;
}
```

Problem 5.7: What is the output of the program below?

```cpp
#include <iostream>
using namespace std;

int main()
{
    const int SIZE = 100;
    int score[ SIZE ], i, min;

    for(i = 0; i < SIZE ; i++)
        score[ i ] = i + 60;

    for(i = 0, min = 2147483647; i < SIZE ; i++)
        if ( score[ i ] < min )
            min = score[i];

    cout << "Minimal value is: " << min << endl;
}
```

Problem 5.8: What is the output of the program below?

```cpp
#include <iostream>
using namespace std;

int main()
{
    const int SIZE = 100;
    double score[ SIZE ];
    int i;

    for(i = 0; i < SIZE ; i++ )
        score[ i ] = 60.0 + i*(1.0);

    for(i = 0; i < SIZE-1 ; i++ )
        if ( score[ i ] == score[ i + 1 ] )
            cout << "Some scores are equal" << endl;

    cout << "No scores are equal" << endl;
}
```

Problem 5.9: What is the output of the program below?

```cpp
#include <iostream>
using namespace std;

int main()
{
    int uninitialized_arrary[3], i;

    for (i = 1; i <= 3; i++)
        uninitialized_arrary[i] = uninitialized_arrary[i - 1] + 5;

    cout << uninitialized_arrary[i] << endl;
}
```

Problem 5.10: What is the output of the program below?

```cpp
#include <iostream>
using namespace std;

int main()
{
    int arr[ 5 ], i;

    for(i = 1; i < 5; i++ )
        arr[ i ] = 3 * i + 1;

    cout << arr[ i ] << endl;
}
```

Problem 5.11: Please implement in C++ that will fill an array arr with 5 values of type float from the keyboard and then output these 5 values separated by newline character (endl).

```cpp
#include <iostream>
using namespace std;

int main()
{
    // Declare array arr here with type float


    // Fill in array arr by reading from the keyboard 5 values



    // Output those 5 values



}
```

Practice 5 – Solution

5.1:   1
49
8
56
56
8
5

5.2:   num = num*10 + str[i]; should be changed to num = num*10 + (str[i]-'0');

5.3:   The program may or may not crash depending on the environment. The string has 18 characters and the index is 18, so str[18] is essentially out of bound.

5.4:   sum of 1 to 5 is: 15

5.5:   Compilation error because of trying to fit 5 integers into an array with 4 spaces for integers.

5.6:   sum of 1 to 5 is: 15

           <u>**Note:**</u> It does not matter how many spaces are in [   ].

5.7:   Minimal value is: 60

5.8:   No scores are equal

5.9:   This program will either crash or print random values because index is out of bound. Array in C++ starts at index 0. uninitialized_arrary[3] references the 4th element in the array, uninitialized_arrary[3] = uninitialized_arrary[2] + 5 might crash the program. Besides, uninitialized_arrary should be initialized.

5.10:   After exiting the for-loop, i has a value of 5. cout << arr[5] will reference arr[5] that causes the program to crash or prints random values because it references the 6th element in an array that only has 5 elements.

5.11:
```cpp
#include <iostream>
using namespace std;

int main()
{
    // Declare array arr here with type float
    float arr[5];

    // Fill in array arr by reading from the keyboard 5 values
    for (int i = 0; i<5; i++)
        cin >> arr[i];

    // Output those 5 values
    for (int i = 0; i<5; i++)
        cout << arr[i] << endl;
}
```

Practice 6 – 1D Array, 2D Array, and C-String

Problem 6.1: What is the output of the program below?

```
#include <iostream>
using namespace std;

int main()
{
    int a[10];

    cout << &a << endl << &a[0] << endl << &a[1] << endl;
    cout << &a[2] << endl << &a[3] << endl << &a[4] << endl;
}
```

Problem 6.2: What is the output of the program below?

```
#include <iostream>
using namespace std;

int main()
{
    const int SIZE = 3;
    int arr[SIZE][SIZE] = { {1,2,3}, {4,5,6}, {7,8,9} };

    for(int i = 0 ; i < SIZE ; i++ )
    {
        for(int j = 0 ; j < SIZE ; j++ )
            cout << arr[ i ][ j ];
        cout << endl;
    }
}
```

Problem 6.3: Similar to Problem #6.2, but this time please declare a 3 by 3 integer array arr, fill it with any integer values from keyboard, and print these 9 numbers on the console output.

```
#include <iostream>
using namespace std;

int sum3numbers(int a[])
{
    return (a[0] + a[1] + a[2]);
}

int main()
{
    int x[ 3 ] = {1, 2, 3};
    cout << sum3numbers( x ) << endl;
}
```

```
#include <iostream>
using namespace std;

int sum3numbers(int a )
{
    return (a[0] + a[1] + a[2]);
}

int main()
{
    int x[ 3 ] = {1, 2, 3};
    cout << sum3numbers( x ) << endl;
}
```

Problem 6.6: What is the output of the program below?

```cpp
#include <iostream>
using namespace std;

//Adding 2 polynomials: 6x^3 + 3x^2 + 2x + 1  and  9x^3 + 15x^2 + 299

int main()
{
    const int SIZE = 4;
    int poly1[] = {1, 2, 3, 6};
    int poly2[] = {299, 0, 15, 9};
    int result[ SIZE ], i;

    for(i = 0 ; i < SIZE ; i++)
        result[ i ] = poly1[ i ] + poly2[ i ];

    cout << "result is: ";

    for(i = SIZE-1 ; i > 0; i--)
        cout << result[i] << "X^" << i << " + ";

    cout << result[0] << endl;
}
```

Problem 6.7: What is the output of the program below?

```cpp
#include <iostream>
using namespace std;

int sumNnumbers(int a[], int N )
{
    int sum, i;

    for(i = 0, sum = 0 ; i < N ; i++ )
        sum = sum + a[ i ] ;

    return sum;
}

int main()
{
    const int SIZE = 100;
    int x[ SIZE ];

    for(int i = 0 ; i < SIZE ; i++)
        x[ i ] = 1;

    cout << sumNnumbers(x, SIZE) << endl;
}
```

Problem 6.8: Please write a function called arrayIntegerDivision (return type is void). The requirement is that if divisor is ZERO, then we output "Cannot divide by zero!" and do nothing (return back to main function). Otherwise, we divide every element in the array by the divisor.

```cpp
#include <iostream>
using namespace std;

// <put arrayIntegerDivision codes here...>




int main()
{
    const int SIZE = 10;
    int x[ SIZE ] = { 2, 4, 6, 8, 10, 12, 14, 16, 18, 20 };
    int divisor = 2;

    arrayIntegerDivision(x, SIZE, divisor); // Write the parameter list

    // based on the variables

    // we passed in….
    for(int i = 0; i< SIZE ; i++ )
        cout << x[i] << endl;
}
```

Problem 6.9: If the following program doesn't compile, why not? If it does compile, what is the output when it is run?

```cpp
#include <iostream>
using namespace std;

void arrayIntegerDivision(const int x[],int n, int y)
{
    if(y == 0)
    {
        cout << "Cannot divide by zero!" << endl;
        return ;
    }

    for(int i = 0 ; i < n ; i++ )
        x[ i ] = x[ i ] / y;
}

int main()
{
    const int SIZE = 10;
    int x[ SIZE ] = { 2, 4, 6, 8, 10, 12, 14, 16, 18, 20 };
    int y = 2;

    arrayIntegerDivision(x, SIZE, y);

    for(int i = 0; i< SIZE ; i++ )
        cout << x[i] << endl;
}
```

Problem 6.10: Is there any compilation error in the following program?

```cpp
#include <iostream>
using namespace std;

void arrayIntegerDivision(const int x[],int n, int y)
{
    cout << "Inside arrayIntegerdivision function..." << endl;

    for(int i = 0 ; i < n ; i++)
        cout << x[ i ] / y << endl;
}

int main()
{
    const int SIZE = 10;
    int x[ SIZE ] = { 2, 4, 6, 8, 10, 12, 14, 16, 18, 20 };
    int y = 2;

    arrayIntegerDivision(x, SIZE, y);

    cout << "Back to main function..." << endl;

    for(int i = 0 ; i < SIZE ; i++)
        cout << x[ i ] << endl;
}
```

Problem 6.11: Please implement a function called SearchArray. It takes as input an integer array, the size of the array, and an integer we want to search for. For example, SearchArray(x, 100, 5) means we want to search for the integer 5 in array x. SearchArray should return a boolean value true or false to let the user know whether the integer exists in array x or not.

```cpp
#include <iostream>
using namespace std;

// implement SearchArray here….
bool SearchArray(const int x[],int n, int value)
{



}
int main()
{
    const int SIZE = 1000;
    int x[ SIZE ], i;

    // Fill in the array with some values....
    for(i = 0 ; i < SIZE ; i++)
        x[ i ] = i*i + i + 1;

    if( SearchArray(x, SIZE, 9901) )
        cout << "Found 9901!\n";

    if( SearchArray(x, SIZE, 8801) )
        cout << "Found 8801!\n";
}
```

```cpp
#include <iostream>
using namespace std;

// We can use int a[3][3] or int a[][3], but not a[][]
void displayArray(int a[3][3],int N)
{
    int i,j;

    for(i = 0 ; i < N ; i++ )
    {
        for(j = 0 ; j < N ; j++ )
            cout << a[ i ][ j ];
        cout << endl;
    }
}

int main()
{
    const int SIZE = 3;
    int a[SIZE][SIZE] = { {1,2,3}, {4,5,6}, {7,8,9} };

    displayArray(a, SIZE);
}
```

Problem 6.13: What is the output of the program below?

```cpp
#include <iostream>
using namespace std;

void swap(int x[],int N)
{
    int temp;
    for(int i = 0; i < N/2 ; i++ )
    {
        temp = x[ i ];
        x[ i ] = x[ N-i-1 ];
        x[ N-i-1 ] = temp;
        // cout << "Swapping between " << i << " and " << N-i-1 << endl;
    }
}

int main()
{
    const int SIZE = 10;
    int x[ SIZE ] = { 10, 9, 8, 7, 6, 5, 4, 3, 2, 1 };
    int i;

    swap(x, SIZE);

    for(int i = 0 ; i < SIZE ; i++)
        cout << x[i] << endl;
}
```

Problem 6.14: What is the output of the program below?

```cpp
#include <iostream>
#include <string>
#include <cassert>
using namespace std;

// Return the position of the first element that is not equal to the one
// that follows it.   Return −1 if there are no such elements.
int findFirstNotEqual(const string a[], int n)
{
    for (int k = 0; k < n-1; k++)
        if (a[k] != a[k+1])
            return k;
     return -1;
}

int main()
{
    string h[5] = { "abc", "abc", "abc", "abe", "abf" };

    assert(findFirstNotEqual(h, 5) == 2);
    assert(findFirstNotEqual(h, 4) == 2);
    assert(findFirstNotEqual(h, 3) == -1);
    assert(findFirstNotEqual(h, 2) == -1);
    assert(findFirstNotEqual(h, 1) == -1);
    assert(findFirstNotEqual(h, 0) == -1);

    cout << "All tests succeeded" << endl;
}
```

Problem 6.15: Please try various character (from a to z) to see what is the output of this program.

```cpp
#include <iostream>
#include <string>
using namespace std;

int main()
{
    string fruits[10] = {   "Apple","Banana","Cherry","DoubleCoconut",
                            "Elderberry","FingerLime","Grapefruit",
                            "Hackberry","IceCreamBean","JellyPalm"};
    char selection;
    do
    {
        cout << "What do you want to eat?" << endl;
        for(int i=0;i<10;i++)
            cout << "(" << (char)('a'+i) << ") " << fruits[i] << endl;

        cout << "(q) quit" << endl;
        cout << "Selection is ? " ;

        cin >> selection;

        if((selection>='a') && (selection <= 'j'))
        {
            cout << "You selected " << fruits[ selection-'a' ] ;

            for(int i=0;i<1000000000;i++); // pause...
        }
        else if(selection == 'q') ;
        else cout << "Please enter character a to j or q to exit.";

        cout << endl << endl;

    }while(selection!='q');
}
```

Problem 6.16: What is the output of the program below?

```cpp
#include <iostream>
#include <string>
using namespace std;

int main()
{
    string fruits[10]= {"Banana","Cherry","DoubleCoconut",
                        "Elderberry","FingerLime","Grapefruit",
                        "Hackberry","IceCreamBean","JellyPalm","Apple"};

    string smallest = fruits[0];
    int smallest_index = 0;

    for(int i=1;i<10;i++)
    {
        if( fruits[i] < smallest)
        {
            smallest = fruits[i];
            smallest_index = i;
        }
    }

    cout << "The index for the smallest fruits string is at "
         << smallest_index << endl;

    if( smallest == "apple" )
        cout << "Found apple!" << endl;
}
```

Problem 6.17: What is the output of the program below?

```cpp
#include <iostream>
using namespace std;

int main()
{
    char str1[ ]  = "C++";
    char str2[ ]  = {"C++"};
    char str3[ ]  = {"C++\0"};
    char str4[4] = "C++";
    char str5[100000] = "C++";
    char str6[ ]  = {'C', '+', '+'};

    cout << str1 << endl << str2 << endl << str3 << endl;
    cout << str4 << endl << str5 << endl << str6 << endl;
}
```

Problem 6.18: If the following program doesn't compile, why not? If it does compile, what is the output when it is run?

```cpp
#include <iostream>
using namespace std;

int main()
{
    char str[14];
    str = "Hello World!\n";

    cout << str << endl;
}
```

```cpp
#include <iostream>
using namespace std;

int mystrlen(const char str[])
{
    int len=0;
    // What if someone forgot to set '\0' in str?
    while(str[len] != '\0' )
        len++;
    return len;
}

int main()
{
    char str[4] = "C++";
    cout << mystrlen(str) << endl;
}
```

```cpp
#include <iostream>
using namespace std;

void mystrcpy(const char str1[], const char str2[])
{
    int len=0;
    while(str2[len] != '\0')
        str1[len]=str2[len++];
}

int main()
{
    char str1[9] = "Practice";
    char str2[9] = "Problems";

    cout << str1 << endl << str2 << endl;
    mystrcpy(str1,str2);
    cout << str1 << endl << str2 << endl;
}
```

Practice 6 – Solution

6.1: 6 different addresses should be printed on the console output. The idea is to show that array has continuous addresses for successive elements.

6.2: 123

456

789

6.3:
```cpp
#include <iostream>
using namespace std;

int main()
{
    const int SIZE = 3;
    int arr[SIZE][SIZE];

    for (int i = 0; i < SIZE; i++)
        for (int j = 0; j < SIZE; j++)
            cin >> arr[i][j];

    for (int i = 0; i < SIZE; i++)
    {
        for (int j = 0; j < SIZE; j++)
            cout << arr[i][j];
        cout << endl;
    }
}
```

6.4: 6

6.5: Compilation error because an array (the beginning address of an array) cannot be assigned to an integer variable.

6.6: result is: $15X^3 + 18X^2 + 2X^1 + 300$

6.7: 100

6.8:
```cpp
#include <iostream>
using namespace std;

void arrayIntegerDivision(int x[], int n, int y)
{
    if (y == 0)
    {
        cout << "Cannot divide by zero!" << endl;
        return;
    }

    for (int i = 0; i < n; i++)
        x[i] = x[i] / y;
}

int main()
{
    const int SIZE = 10;
    int x[SIZE] = { 2, 4, 6, 8, 10, 12, 14, 16, 18, 20 };
    int y = 2;

    arrayIntegerDivision(x, SIZE, y);

    for (int i = 0; i< SIZE; i++)
        cout << x[i] << endl;
}
```

6.9: Compilation error because the array x is declared as "const int" meaning that the elements of the array cannot be changed. Thus x[i] = x[i] / y; causes the compilation error.

6.10: No compilation error.

6.11:
```cpp
#include <iostream>
using namespace std;

// implement SearchArray here....
bool SearchArray(const int x[], int n, int value)
{
    for (int i = 0; i<n; i++)
        if (x[i] == value)
                return true;
    return false;
}
int main()
{
    const int SIZE = 1000;
    int x[SIZE], i;

    // Fill in the array with some values....
    for (i = 0; i < SIZE; i++)
        x[i] = i*i + i + 1;

    if (SearchArray(x, SIZE, 9901))
        cout << "Found 9901!\n";

    if (SearchArray(x, SIZE, 8801))
        cout << "Found 8801!\n";
}
```

6.12:   123

456

789

6.13:   1

2

3

4

5

6

7

8

9

10

6.14:   All tests succeeded

6.15:   Depending on the inputs, the outputs are different. For example, an input 'a' will see "You selected Apple" as the output.

6.16:   The index for the smallest fruits string is at 9

6.17:   C++
              C++
              C++
              C++
              C++
              C++   ++

Note: the last line in the outputs should contain some random characters because the c-string does not stop until it accidentally finds '\0' in the memory that follows the beginning address of the array.

6.18:   Compilation error. The proper way is to use strcpy() function to copy the contents of the constant string to str array instead of trying to change the address of a static array to point to the address of a constant string.

6.19:   3

6.20:   Compilation error because str1 and str2 arrays inside mystrcpy() function are declared as const, and str1[len]=str2[len++] will try to change the elements in the const array str1. Removing "const" in front of str1 solves the problem.

Practice Midterm 2

Problem	Maximal Possible Points	Received
1	10	
2	10	
3	10	
4	10	
5	10	
6	15	
Total Score	65	

Problem #1: The Collatz conjecture states that when taking any natural number n, if n is even, set n = n /2. If n is odd, set n = 3n + 1. Repeat this process until n is equal to 1. The conjecture states that no matter what number you start with, you will always reach 1. Please fill in the blanks below to complete the program. Assume n is from 0~100.

```cpp
#include <iostream>
using namespace std;

int main()
{
    int n,count;
    while(cin >> n && n > 0)
    {

        count = 0;

        while(                      )
        {




        }
        cout << "There are " << count;
        cout << " numbers being generated!" << endl;
    }
}
```

Problem #2: An National Spying Agency worker has found some patterns in encoded messages such that when 2 consecutive encoded messages (shorter than 9 characters) with complementing 0s and 1s show up, the real message, though encoded, follows. He needs your help to write the following program for him to check for such patterns. For example, "1111" and "0000" are complementary to each other, while "1011" and "0101" are not complementary to each other.

```cpp
#include <iostream>
#include <cstring>
using namespace std;

bool isComplement(char row1[],int len1,char row2[],int len2)
{



}

int main()
{
    char row1[9],row2[9];
    cin >> row1 >> row2;
    if(isComplement(row1,strlen(row1),row2,strlen(row2)))
        cout << "They are complementary to each other!" << endl;
    else
        cout << "Life is tough!!" << endl;
}
```

Problem #3: An old trick to encrypt messages is to embed the real message into random characters in a certain pattern. Suppose that we know the pattern to decode is to extract the 1st, 3rd, 5th, 7th, …characters out of the encoded messages. For example, "BAAANPALNEA" can be decoded as "BANANA". Please complete such function below. Assume that encodedMsg will always have length greater than 1.

```cpp
#include <iostream>
#include <cstring>
using namespace std;

void solvePuzzle( char encodedMsg[] ,char decodedMsg[] )
{




}

int main()
{
    char encodedMsg[] = "BAAANPALNEA";
    char decodedMsg[100];

    solvePuzzle(encodedMsg,decodedMsg);

    cout << "The decoded message is: " << decodedMsg << endl;
}
```

Problem #4: What is the output of the program below?

```cpp
#include <iostream>
#include <cstring>
using namespace std;

bool findTriple(char str[])
{
    int i;

    bool foundTripleZero = false;
    for(i = 1 ; i < strlen(str)-2 ; i++ )
    {
        if(foundTripleZero == true)
            foundTripleZero = false;

        else if( ( str[i] == str[i+1]) && (str[i+1] == str[i+2]) )
            foundTripleZero = true;
    }
    return foundTripleZero;
}

int main()
{
    cout << findTriple("01110");
    cout << findTriple("00110");
    cout << findTriple("00010");
    cout << findTriple("10001");
    cout << endl;
}
```

(1) 0000
(2) 0001
(3) 0010
(4) 0011
(5) 1000
(6) 1001
(7) 1010
(8) 1011
(9) 1100

Problem #5: You work in a math lab that requires finding root x for a function f(x) such that f(x) = 0. Please complete the following findRoot function without using any extra variables. You need to check if the values from x array can make f(x) equal to zero and if so, store such value in the root array and update m to signal how many values are in the root array. findRoot() should return true if there is at least a value in x array such that f(x) is equal to 0.

```cpp
#include <iostream>
using namespace std;
int f(int x)
{
    // x^3 - 2x^2 - 5x + 6
    return (x*x*x-2*x*x-5*x+6);
}
bool findRoot(int x[], int n, int root[], int &m)
{
    bool foundRoot = false;
    int i;
    m = 0;




}

int main()
{
    int x[31],root[31];
    int n = 31,m = 0;

    for(int i=0;i < n ; i++)
        x[i] = i - 15;

    if(findRoot(x,n,root,m))
        cout << "Found root for f(x)" << endl;
}
```

Problem #6: You are to write a program to control a robot to move left and right. The up and down keys, though can be accepted by the program, are no-op, but they are still valid keys in the commands. Your goal is to complete the function executeCommands such that the program
(1) Checks if the keys are valid (L / R / U / D) and if any of keys in the string cmdStr are not valid, return -1 without further processing.
(2) Updates points if the robot lands on a specific position as determined by updatePoints() function. The starting point (the initial value in pos in executeCommands function) can get points right away. Even if the robot does not move because the command is U or D, the robot can still get points by staying at that position.
(3) Update position of the robot by adding 1 to pos if the key is R, subtracting 1 to pos if the key is L, and do nothing if the key is U or D.
(4) After you process a valid key, update points.
(5) Return the points back from executeCommands function.

You cannot use any extra variables or arrays in executeCommands function.

To verify the correctness of your program, the output in the completed program should be
0
-1
-1
9

Assume the program below already has the necessary headers:
#include <iostream>
#include <string>
using namespace std;

```cpp
int updatePoints(int pos)
{
    if( pos == 3 ) return 1;
    if( pos == 1 ) return -1;
    if( pos == 5 ) return 2;
    if( pos == 2 ) return -2;
    return 0;
}
int executeCommands(string cmdStr, int pos, int points)
{
    int i;




}
int main()
{
    string command1 = "LULDR";
    string command2 = "LRDULRDUXX";
    string command3 = "UUDDLLRRBA";
    string command4 = "DDURDDUR";

    cout << executeCommands(command1, 0 , 0) << endl;
    cout << executeCommands(command2, 1 , 1) << endl;
    cout << executeCommands(command3, 2 , 2) << endl;
    cout << executeCommands(command4, 3 , 3) << endl;
}
```

Practice Midterm 2 – Solution

1:
```cpp
#include <iostream>
using namespace std;

int main()
{
    int n, count;
    while (cin >> n && n > 0) {
        count = 0;
        while (n != 1) {
            if (n % 2 == 0) n /= 2;
            else n = 3 * n + 1;
            count++;
        }
        cout << "There are " << count;
        cout << " numbers being generated!" << endl;
    }
}
```

2:
```cpp
#include <iostream>
#include <cstring>
using namespace std;

bool isComplement(char row1[], int len1, char row2[], int len2)
{
    if (len1 != len2)
        return false;

    for (int i = 0; i < len1; i++)
        if (row1[i] == row2[i])
            return false;

    return true;
}

int main()
{
    char row1[9], row2[9];
    cin >> row1 >> row2;
    if (isComplement(row1, strlen(row1), row2, strlen(row2)))
        cout << "They are complementary to each other!" << endl;
    else
        cout << "Life is tough!!" << endl;
}
```

3:

```cpp
#include <iostream>
#include <cstring>
using namespace std;

void solvePuzzle(char encodedMsg[], char decodedMsg[])
{
    int i, j;

    for (i = 0, j = 0; i < strlen(encodedMsg); i += 2, j++)
        decodedMsg[j] = encodedMsg[i];

    decodedMsg[j] = 0;
}

int main()
{
    char encodedMsg[] = "BAAANPALNEA";
    char decodedMsg[100];

    solvePuzzle(encodedMsg, decodedMsg);

    cout << "The decoded message is: " << decodedMsg << endl;
}
```

4:   (1)

5:

```cpp
bool findRoot(int x[], int n, int root[], int &m)
{
    bool foundRoot = false;
    int i;
    m = 0;
    for (i = 0; i<n; i++)
        if (f(x[i]) == 0) {
            root[m] = x[i];
            m++;
            foundRoot = true;
        }
    return foundRoot;
}
```

6:

```cpp
int executeCommands(string cmdStr, int pos, int points)
{
    int i;

    for (i = 0; i < cmdStr.size(); i++)
        if (cmdStr[i] != 'U' && cmdStr[i] != 'D' &&
            cmdStr[i] != 'L' && cmdStr[i] != 'R')
            return -1;

    points = points + updatePoints(pos);

    for (i = 0; i < cmdStr.size(); i++)
    {
        if (cmdStr[i] == 'L') pos--;
        else if (cmdStr[i] == 'R') pos++;

        points = points + updatePoints(pos);
    }
    return points;
}
```

Practice 7 – Array and Cstring

Problem 7.1: What is the output of the program below?

```cpp
#include <iostream>
using namespace std;

int mystrcmp(const char str1[],const char str2[])
{
    int len1 = 0, len2 = 0;

    while((str1[len1] == str2[len2]) &&
          (str1[len1] != '\0') &&
          (str2[len2] != '\0' ))
    {
            len1++;
            len2++;
    }

    if (str1[len1] > str2[len2])
            return 1;
    else if ( str1[len1] < str2[len2] )
            return -1;
    return 0;
}

int main()
{
    char str1[14] = "CS31";
    char str2[14] = "CS32";

    cout << mystrcmp(str1,str2) << endl;
}
```

Problem 7.2: What is the output of the program below?

```cpp
#include <iostream>
#include <cstring>
using namespace std;

void mystrcat(char str1[],const char str2[])
{
    // str1 needs to have enough free space, otherwise the program might crash
    int i, j;

    for(i = strlen(str1), j=0 ; j < strlen(str2) ; i++ , j++)
        str1[i] = str2[j];
    str1[i] = '\0';
}

int main()
{
    char str1[14] = "CS31";
    char str2[14] = "CS32";

    cout << "str1 has length: " << strlen(str1) << endl;
    cout << "str2 has length: " << strlen(str2) << endl;

    mystrcat(str1,str2);

    cout << str1 << endl;
    cout << str2 << endl;
}
```

```cpp
// When using strcpy in Visual C++, you might encounter the following compilation
// error: error C4996: 'strcpy': This function or variable may be unsafe. Consider using
// strcpy_s instead. To disable deprecation, use _CRT_SECURE_NO_WARNINGS.
// We can bypass this error by putting the following line at the beginning of the program.
#define _CRT_SECURE_NO_WARNINGS
```

```cpp
#include <iostream>
#include <cstring>
using namespace std;

int main()
{
    char str1[14] = "CS31";
    char str2[14] = "CS32";

    cout << "str1 has length: " << strlen(str1) << endl;
    cout << "str2 has length: " << strlen(str2) << endl;

    strcat(str1,str2);
    cout << str1 << endl << str2 << endl;

    strcpy(str1,str2);
    cout << str1 << endl << str2 << endl;

    if(strcmp(str1,str2) == 0)
        cout << "string 1 and string 2 are equal!\n";
    else
        cout << "string 1 and string 2 are not equal!\n";
}
```

```cpp
#include <iostream>
#include <cstring>
using namespace std;

int main()
{
    char str[5] = "CS31";

    strcat(str," string explosion!!!!!!!!!!");

    cout << str << endl;
}
```

Problem 7.5: What is the output of the program below?

```cpp
#include <iostream>
#include <cstring>
using namespace std;

int main()
{
    char output[1000];

    strcpy( output, "The learning curve for C++ ");
    strcat( output, "is steep!");

    cout << output << endl;
}
```

Problem 7.6: For the following program, if the user inputs "Hello World" twice, what is the output of the program?

```cpp
#include <iostream>
#include <cstring>
using namespace std;

int main()
{
    char str[100];
    cin >> str;
    cout << str << endl;
    cin.ignore(1000,'\n');

    cin.getline(str,100);
    cout << str << endl;
}
```

Problem 7.7: Please write a C++ program to get input string "hello world" from the user and write a function to convert every letter in the string to upper case letter (by using the toupper() function) and output such string to the console.

```cpp
#include <iostream>
#include <cstring>
#include <cctype>
using namespace std;

void convertToUpperCase(char str[])
{




}

int main()
{









}
```

Problem 7.8: What is the output of the program below?

```cpp
#include <iostream>
#include <cstring>
using namespace std;

int main()
{
    char fruits[10][100] = {  "Apple","Banana","Cherry","DoubleCoconut",
                              "Elderberry","FingerLime","Grapefruit",
                              "Hackberry","IceCreamBean","JellyPalm"};

    cout << strlen(fruits[0]) << endl << strlen(fruits[1]) << endl;
    cout << strlen(fruits[2]) << endl << strlen(fruits[3]) << endl;
    cout << strlen(fruits[4]) << endl << strlen(fruits[5]) << endl;
    cout << strlen(fruits[6]) << endl << strlen(fruits[7]) << endl;
    cout << strlen(fruits[8]) << endl << strlen(fruits[9]) << endl;

    char selected_fruits[200];

    strcpy(selected_fruits,fruits[0]);
    strcat(selected_fruits,fruits[1]);
    strcat(selected_fruits,fruits[2]);

    cout << selected_fruits << endl;

    if( strcmp(selected_fruits, "AppleBananaCherry") == 0)
        cout << "AppleBananaCherry!" << endl;
}
```

```cpp
#include <iostream>
#include <cstring>
using namespace std;

int main()
{
    char fruits[10][100] = { "Apple","Banana","Cherry","DoubleCoconut",
                             "Elderberry","FingerLime","Grapefruit",
                             "Hackberry","IceCreamBean","JellyPalm"};

    for(int i = 0 ; i < strlen(fruits[0]) ; i++ )
        fruits[0][ i ] = tolower( fruits[0][ i ] );

    cout << (fruits[0][4]=toupper(fruits[0][4]));

    if( isupper( fruits[1][0] ) )
        cout << fruits[1][0];

    if( isupper( fruits[2][0] ) )
        cout << fruits[2][0];

    if( isalpha( fruits[3][0] ) )
        cout << fruits[3][0];

    if( ! isdigit( fruits[8][0] ) )
        cout << fruits[8][0];

    if( islower( fruits[8][1] ) )
        cout << (fruits[8][1]=toupper(fruits[8][1]));

    cout << endl;
}
```

Problem 7.10: Please write a function called replaceUpperCaseLetters (return type is void). The function takes as input a C-style string (char array) and the function will replace all upper case letters by hyphens.

```cpp
#include <iostream>
#include <cstring>
using namespace std;

void replaceUpperCaseLetters(char str[])
{




}

int main()
{
    char str[] = "C++C++C++C++C++";

    replaceUpperCaseLetters(str);

    cout << str << endl;
}
```

Problem 7.11: A palindrome is a sequence of characters that reads the same front to end as it does end to front. Examples are: 121 / aabaa / 123321 / abzba. Please try various sequence of characters to see what is the output of this program.

```cpp
#include <iostream>
#include <cstring>
using namespace std;

bool isPalindrome(char str[])
{
    int strLen = strlen(str);
    int i,j;
    char reverse[1000];
    for(i=strLen-1, j=0;i >= 0; i--, j++)
        reverse[ j ] = str[ i ];
    reverse[j] = 0;

    return !strcmp(str , reverse);
}

int main()
{
    const int SIZE = 1000;
    char str[SIZE];

    cin >> str;

    if(isPalindrome(str))
        cout << "It is a palindrome." << endl;
    else
        cout << "It is not a palindrome." << endl;
}
```

Problem 7.12: Please rewrite the program in Problem 7.11 by using C++ string.

```cpp
#include <iostream>
#include <string>
using namespace std;

bool isPalindrome(string str)
{



}

int main()
{
    string str;

    cin >> str;

    if(isPalindrome(str))
        cout << "It is a palindrome." << endl;
    else
        cout << "It is not a palindrome." << endl;
}
```

Practice 7 – Solution

7.1:   -1

7.2:   str1 has length: 4

str2 has length: 4

CS31CS32

CS32

7.3:   str1 has length: 4

str2 has length: 4

CS31CS32

CS32

CS32

CS32

string 1 and string 2 are equal!

7.4:   The program should crash as it copies more than 5 characters into str array.

7.5:   The learning curve for C++ is steep!

7.6:   Hello

Hello World

7.7:

```cpp
#include <iostream>
#include <cstring>
#include <cctype>
using namespace std;

void convertToUpperCase(char str[])
{
    // Please use toupper() function.
    for (int i = 0; i<strlen(str); i++)
        str[i] = toupper(str[i]);
}

int main()
{
    char str[1000];
    cin.getline(str, 999);
    convertToUpperCase(str);
    cout << str << endl;
}
```

7.8:   5

6

6

13

10

10

10

9

12

9

AppleBananaCherry

AppleBananaCherry!

7.9:   EBCDIC

7.10:
```cpp
#include <iostream>
#include <cstring>
using namespace std;

void replaceUpperCaseLetters(char str[])
{
    for (int i = 0; i<strlen(str); i++)
        if (isupper(str[i]))
            str[i] = '-';
}

int main()
{
    char str[] = "C++C++C++C++C++";

    replaceUpperCaseLetters(str);

    cout << str << endl;
}
```

7.11: Depending on the inputs, the outputs are different. For example, an input '45654' will see "It is a palindrome." as the output.

7.12:
```cpp
#include <iostream>
#include <string>
using namespace std;

bool isPalindrome(string str)
{
    string reverse = "";
    for (int i = str.size() - 1; i >= 0; i--)
        reverse += str[i];
    return str == reverse;
}

int main()
{
    string str;

    cin >> str;

    if (isPalindrome(str))
        cout << "It is a palindrome." << endl;
    else
        cout << "It is not a palindrome." << endl;
}
```

Practice 8 - Pointers

> Problem 8.1: If the following program doesn't compile, why not? If it does compile, what is the output when it is run?

```cpp
#include <iostream>
using namespace std;

int main()
{
    int *p;
    *p = 100;

    cout << p << endl;
    cout << *p << endl;
}
```

> Problem 8.2: What is the output of the program below?

```cpp
#include <iostream>
using namespace std;

int main()
{
    int *p = new int;
    *p = 100;

    cout << p << endl;
    cout << *p << endl;

    delete p;
}
```

Problem 8.3: What is the output of the program below?

```cpp
#include <iostream>
using namespace std;

int main()
{
    int *p = new int;
    *p = 100;

    cout << p << endl;
    cout << *p << endl;

    *p = *p + 7;     // What about p = p + 7 ?

    cout << p << endl;
    cout << *p << endl;

    delete p;
}
```

Problem 8.4: What is the output of the program below if the input is an integer 1000?

```cpp
#include <iostream>
using namespace std;

int main()
{
    int a;

    int *p = &a;     // This is a shorthand for:
                     // int *p;   p = &a;

    cin >> *p;

    cout << *p << endl;
}
```

```cpp
#include <iostream>
using namespace std;

int main()
{
    int *a,*b,*c,*d,*e,*f,*g,*h,*i,*j,*k;

    *a=*b=*c=*d=*e=*f=*g=*h=*i=*j=*k=2;

    cout << *a+*b+*c+*d+*e+*f+*g+*h+*i+*j+*k << endl;
}
```

```cpp
#include <iostream>
using namespace std;

int main()
{
    const double pi = 3.141592653589793;
    double *p = &pi;

    *p = 2;

    cout << *p << endl;
}
```

```cpp
#include <iostream>
using namespace std;

int main()
{
    int x = (9 / 10) * 10;

    cout << *(&x) << endl;
}
```

```cpp
#include <iostream>
using namespace std;

int main()
{
    int x = 100;
    int *px = &x;

    *px++;

    // What about (*px)++; ?

    cout << *px << endl;
}
```

```cpp
#include <iostream>
using namespace std;

int main()
{
    int value = 1000;
    int *p = &value;
    int *q;
    q = &value;

    cout << "Address of value is: " << &value << endl;
    cout << "Value of value is: " << value << endl;

    cout << "Address of p is: " << p << endl;
    cout << "Value of p is: " << *p << endl;

    cout << "Address of p is: " << q << endl;
    cout << "Value of p is: " << *q << endl;
}
```

Problem 8.10: What is the output of the program below?

```cpp
#include <iostream>
using namespace std;

int main()
{
    int x[5] = {1,2,3,4,5};
    int *p = x;    // same as int *p = &x[0];
    // x is the beginning address of an array
    // so the above is the same as:
    // int *p;    p = x;

    cout << "*p is x[0]" << endl;
    cout << *p << endl;
    cout << p << endl;

    cout << "*p++ returns *p and then do p++" << endl;
    cout << *p++ << endl;
    cout << p << endl;

    cout << "*(p++) is the same as *p++" << endl;
    cout << *(p++) << endl;
    cout << p << endl;

    cout << "(*p)++ means adding 1 to (*p) which is x[2] here." << endl;
    cout << (*p)++ << endl;
    cout << p << endl; // address does not change

    for(int i=0;i<5;i++)
        cout << x[i] << " ";
    cout << endl;
}
```

```cpp
#include <iostream>
using namespace std;

int main()
{
    int v1 = 99, v2=1000;

    cout << "Address of v1 is: " << &v1 << endl;
    cout << "Address of v2 is: " << &v2 << endl;
    cout << "Value of v1 is: " << v1 << endl;
    cout << "Value of v2 is: " << v2 << endl;
    cout << "---------------------------- " << endl;

    int *p1 = &v1;
    int *p2 = &v2;

    cout << "Address of p is: " << p1 << endl;
    cout << "Address of p is: " << p2 << endl;
    cout << "Value of p is: " << *p1 << endl;
    cout << "Value of p is: " << *p2 << endl;
    cout << "---------------------------- " << endl;

    *p1 = *p2;

    cout << "After running *p1 = *p2 ..." << endl;

    cout << "Address of v1 is: " << &v1 << endl;
    cout << "Address of v2 is: " << &v2 << endl;
    cout << "Value of v1 is: " << v1 << endl;
    cout << "Value of v2 is: " << v2 << endl;
    cout << "---------------------------- " << endl;

    *p1 = 199;
    v2  = 30000;

    cout << "After running *p1 = 199 and v2 = 30000" << endl;

    cout << "Address of p1 is: " << p1 << endl;
    cout << "Address of p2 is: " << p2 << endl;
```

```cpp
    cout << "Value of p1 is: " << *p1 << endl;
    cout << "Value of p2 is: " << *p2 << endl;
    cout << "----------------------------- " << endl;

    p1 = p2;

    cout << "After running p1 = p2 ..." << endl;

    cout << "Address of v1 is: " << &v1 << endl;
    cout << "Address of v2 is: " << &v2 << endl;
    cout << "Value of v1 is: " << v1 << endl;
    cout << "Value of v2 is: " << v2 << endl;

    cout << "Address of p1 is: " << p1 << endl;
    cout << "Address of p2 is: " << p2 << endl;
    cout << "Value of p1 is: " << *p1 << endl;
    cout << "Value of p2 is: " << *p2 << endl;
    cout << "----------------------------- " << endl;
}
```

Problem 8.12: What is the output of the program below?

```cpp
#include <iostream>
using namespace std;

int mystrlen(char *p)
{
    int len=0;
    while(*p++ != '\0')
        len++;
    return len;
}

int main()
{
    char str1[] = "C++";
    char str2[] = "Pointers are very powerful!";
    cout << mystrlen(str1) << endl;
    cout << mystrlen(str2) << endl;
}
```

Problem 8.13: Please use pointers to implement mystrcpy() to copy the c-string pointed to by str2 to the c-string pointed to by str1. Your implementation should make the program produce the following outputs:
C++
Pointers
Pointers
Pointers

```cpp
#include <iostream>
using namespace std;

void mystrcpy(char *str1, char *str2)
{



}

int main()
{
    char str1[15] = "C++";
    char str2[15] = "Pointers";

    cout << str1 << endl << str2 << endl;

    mystrcpy(str1, str2); // copy from str2 to str1

    cout << str1 << endl << str2 << endl;
}
```

Problem 8.14: What is the output of the program below?

```cpp
#include <iostream>
using namespace std;

// int *x is the same as int x[]
bool findValue(int *x, int n, int value)
{
    int i;
    for(i=0;i<n;i++)
    {
        if( *(x+i) == value )
            return true;
        // *(x + i ) is the same as x[i]
    }
    return false;
}

int main()
{
    int x[5] = {1,2,3,4,5};
    int value = 3;

    if(findValue(x,5,value))
        cout << "Found " << value << endl;

}
```

```
#include <iostream>
using namespace std;

int main()
{
    int x = 5, y = 10;
    const int *p = &x;

    cout << *p << endl;

    p = &y;

    cout << *p << endl;
}
```

```
#include <iostream>
using namespace std;

int main()
{
    int x = 5, y = 10;
    const int *p = &x;

    cout << *p << endl;

    *p = 50;

    cout << *p << endl;
}
```

```cpp
#include <iostream>
using namespace std;

int main()
{
    int *p;

    p = new int;

    cout << "*p = " << *p << endl;

    int *q = p;

    cout << "p = " << p << endl;
    cout << "q = " << q << endl;

    delete p;

    *q = 100;

    cout << "*p = " << *p << endl;

    cout << "p = " << p << endl;
    cout << "q = " << q << endl;
}
```

Practice 8 – Solution

8.1: In Visual C++ 2015, it's a compilation error "C4700 uninitialized local variable 'p' used". In GCC version 4.8.4, this program can be compiled and run, but the run will end up as "segmentation fault" (the program will crash). This is because p is never initialized, so p points to an invalid or random memory address. Assigning a value to be stored in an invalid/random memory address is just disastrous.

8.2: The outputs should consist of 2 lines. The first one is a memory address, and the second line is an integer value 100.

8.3: 00389730
100
00389730
107
Note: You should see a different address other than 00389730. As for p = p+7, this adds 7 (size of int) to the memory address stored in p instead of the content of the address stored in p.

8.4: 1000

8.5: In Visual C++ 2015, it's a compilation error "C4700 uninitialized local variable 'a' used". In GCC version 4.8.4, this program can be compiled and run, but the run will end up as "segmentation fault" (the program will crash). This is because a, b, c, d, e, f, g, h, i, j, k are never initialized, so they all point to invalid or random memory addresses. Assigning a value to be stored in an invalid/random memory address is just disastrous.

8.6: Compilation error because a non-constant pointer cannot store the address that's stored in a constant pointer. If this were to be allowed, then the non-constant pointer could modify the constant value in the constant variable pi.

8.7: 0
Note: * and & cancel each other out.

8.8: The output should be a random number. *px++ applies the deferencing operator (*) on the memory address stored in px and then advance the memory address by the size of int. So px now points to a different memory address which has a random value there when dereferenced.

8.9: Address of value is: 0015FB2C
Value of value is: 1000
Address of p is: 0015FB2C
Value of p is: 1000
Address of p is: 0015FB2C
Value of p is: 1000
Note: In your computer, you shall see a different address than 0015FB2C.

8.10:   *p is x[0]
1
0047F898
*p++ returns *p and then do p++
1
0047F89C
*(p++) is the same as *p++
2
0047F8A0
(*p)++ means adding 1 to (*p) which is x[2] here.
3
0047F8A0
1 2 4 4 5
Note: You shall see different memory addresses in your computer.

8.11:   Address of v1 is: 0051FBBC
Address of v2 is: 0051FBB0
Value of v1 is: 99
Value of v2 is: 1000

Address of p is: 0051FBBC
Address of p is: 0051FBB0
Value of p is: 99
Value of p is: 1000

After running *p1 = *p2 ...
Address of v1 is: 0051FBBC
Address of v2 is: 0051FBB0
Value of v1 is: 1000
Value of v2 is: 1000

After running *p1 = 199 and v2 = 30000
Address of p1 is: 0051FBBC
Address of p2 is: 0051FBB0
Value of p1 is: 199
Value of p2 is: 30000

After running p1 = p2 ...
Address of v1 is: 0051FBBC
Address of v2 is: 0051FBB0
Value of v1 is: 199
Value of v2 is: 30000
Address of p1 is: 0051FBB0
Address of p2 is: 0051FBB0
Value of p1 is: 30000
Value of p2 is: 30000

Note: You shall see different memory addresses in your computer.

8.12:   3
27

8.13:
```
void mystrcpy(char *str1, char *str2)
{
      while (*str1++ = *str2++);
}
```

8.14:   Found 3

8.15:   5
10

8.16:   Compilation error because const int *p means that *p cannot be changed, but this still allows p to point to different addresses.

8.17:   In GCC 4.8.4, you might see outputs like this:
*p = 0
p = 0x14fe010   *Note that this address should be different on your computer
q = 0x14fe010
*p = 100
p = 0x14fe010
q = 0x14fe010

In Visual C++ 2015, you might see outputs like this:
*p = -842150451
p = 00819D38
q = 00819D38
Then the program crashes here.

Basically, after people freed the space they newed, they no longer own that space as that space could be taken by some other programs running in the computer. So *q = 100 ended up assigning an integer value 100 to be stored in a space that may be owned by other programs running in the computer, hence infringing other program's memory space (illegal trespassing!!).

Also note that even after freeing the space, the pointers p and q still store the address of that space.

Practice 8v2 – More Pointers

By now, you should have some ideas about what are pointers. Below, I'll explain more about pointers. Suppose we have the following pointer:

int *P;

This means we declare a pointer P of (int *) type such that P can hold address value. The reason P is (int *) type, not (int) type is because P wants to store an address, not an integer.

P has its own address and space and P can store an address value in its space as shown below. 0xcccccccc is the initial value Visual C++ gives to signal that there is nothing stored in P.

```
  P
┌──────────────┐
│ 0xcccccccc   │
└──────────────┘
```

The following program shows you that an initialized pointer P has its own address and has spaces to store an address. Swapping int* P below to char *P gives you different address but the same size. This is because address is the address to find a location in memory and it does not matter if it's int or char. So why do we need to use int* or char*? Because when we use P++ or P = P + 1, we need to know how many bytes to increment to the next address. Assume we use Visual C++ on 32-bit computer, if we have int* P, P++ will increment P by 4 bytes. If we have char* P, P++ will increment P by 1 byte.

```
#include <iostream>
using namespace std;

int main()
{
    int *P;
    cout << "P's address is: " << &P << endl;
    cout << "P's SIZE is: " << sizeof(P) << endl;
}
```

Some people might get the SIZE of P as 4, while others might get the SIZE of P as 8. The difference is from each person's computer and compiler. If you use a 32-bit computer, the SIZE of P is 4 bytes as 4 bytes * (8 bit per byte) = 32 bit. If you use a 64-bit computer with a compiler supporting 64-bit addressing ability, the SIZE of P is 8 bytes as 8 bytes * (8 bit per byte) = 64 bit. That's why you can see the spec of the computer on the market has 32-bit or 64-bit differences in it.

32-bit computer can only allow pointers access up to 4GB of memory because 2^{32} = 4096 MB = 4GB. 64-bit computer can allow pointers access up to 2^{64} bytes which is 2^{44} GB of memory.

Let us dig deeper into pointers. Suppose we have the following program:

```
#include <iostream>
using namespace std;

int main()
{
    int number = 7;
    int *P = &number;
    cout << *P << endl;
}
```

Graphically, below is what it looks like. (When you run the same program on your computer, you'll absolutely see different addresses, but concept is the same).

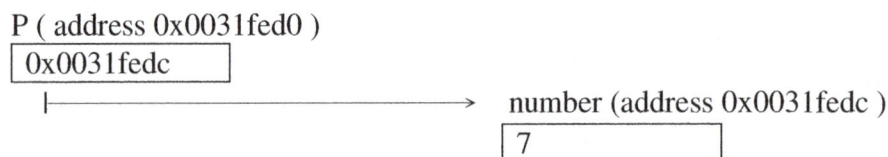

P (address 0x0031fed0)

| 0x0031fedc |

├———————————————————→ number (address 0x0031fedc)

| 7 |

int number = 7; stores an integer value 7 in a variable called "number" at an address 0x0031fedc in memory. int *P = &number; means storing the address of the variable "number" in P. Here, you can see how similar it is between int and int*. int stores an integer value while int* stores an address.

So P stores the address (0x0031fedc) just as number stores the integer 7.
*P is *(0x0031fedc) which is to jump to address 0x0031fedc and get the content from 0x0031fedc. *(0x0031fedc) is just 7.

Suppose we have another program below:
```
#include <iostream>
using namespace std;

int main()
{
    int *P;
    *P = 7;
}
```
In Visual C++, this program cannot be run due to uninitialized pointer error. If we run this program in GCC version 4.8.4, we will get segmentation fault (runtime error). This is because we try to assign the integer 7 to an in-accessible address. In Visual C++, uninitialized pointer will be set an initial value 0xcccccccc to show that it's uninitialized, so when you do *P = 7; it will cause not work.

P (address 0x0031fed0)

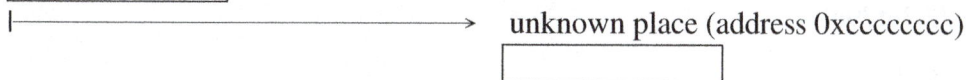

*(0xcccccccc) = 7; will not work. Visual C++ recognizes 0xcccccccc as uninitialized.

In GCC 4.8.4, the initial address pointed to by P could be some random address that accessing such address may or may not cause problems. If you get lucky, it might sometimes work.

P (address 0x0031fed0)

*(Random Address) = 7; may or may not work depending on what that Random Address is.

Now suppose we have the following program:

```
#include <iostream>
using namespace std;
int main()
{
    int arr[5] = {1,2,3,4,5};
    int *a = &arr[0];
    int *b = &arr[1];      // (1)
    a = b;                 // (2)
    for(int i=0;i<5;i++)
        cout << arr[i] << " ";
    cout << endl;
}
```

The output is still 1 2 3 4 5. In other words, a=b did not change the values in arr array.
As we execute the program after (1), below is what the pointers look like:

a (address 0x0036f79c)

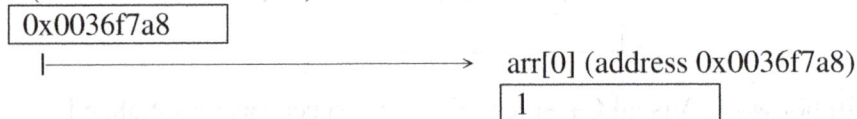

| 0x0036f7a8 |

|————————————————————————→ arr[0] (address 0x0036f7a8)

| 1 |

b (address 0x0036f790)

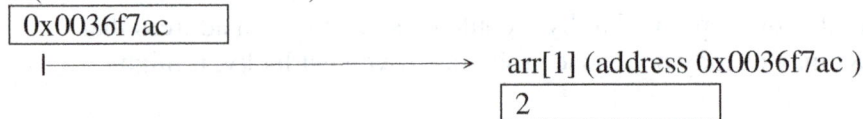

| 0x0036f7ac |

|————————————————————————→ arr[1] (address 0x0036f7ac)

| 2 |

After executing a=b at (2),

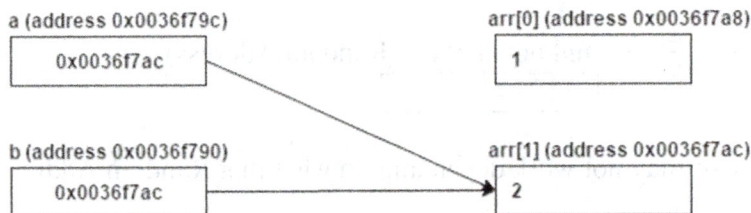

a (address 0x0036f79c)

| 0x0036f7ac |

arr[0] (address 0x0036f7a8)

| 1 |

b (address 0x0036f790)

| 0x0036f7ac |

arr[1] (address 0x0036f7ac)

| 2 |

a=b simply assigns the address stored in b to a without changing arr[0] and arr[1].

Now suppose we have the following program:

```cpp
#include <iostream>
using namespace std;
int main()
{
    int arr[5] = {1,2,3,4,5};
    int *a = &arr[0];
    int *b = &arr[1];         // (1)
    *a = *b;                  // (2)
    for(int i=0;i<5;i++)
        cout << arr[i] << " ";
    cout << endl;
}
```

The output becomes 2 2 3 4 5. In other words, *a=*b did change the values in arr array.
As we execute the program after (1), below is what the pointers look like:

a (address 0x0036f79c)

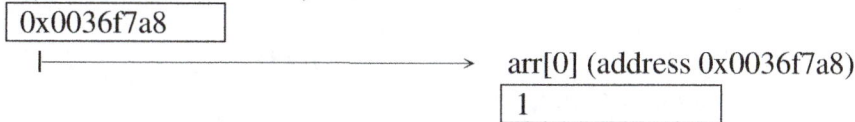

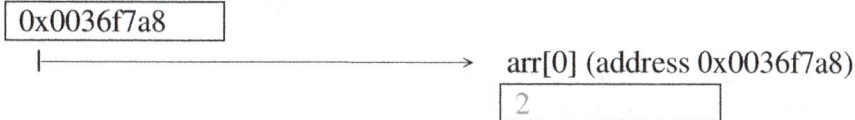

| 0x0036f7a8 |

⊢————————————————————→ arr[0] (address 0x0036f7a8)

| 1 |

b (address 0x0036f790)

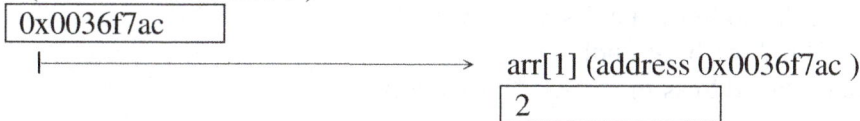

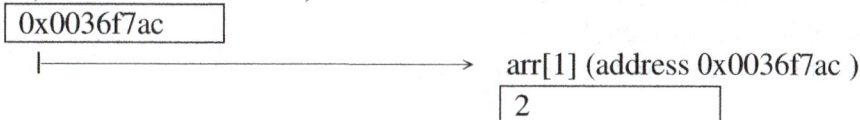

| 0x0036f7ac |

⊢————————————————————→ arr[1] (address 0x0036f7ac)

| 2 |

After executing *a=*b at (2),
a (address 0x0036f79c)

| 0x0036f7a8 |

⊢————————————————————→ arr[0] (address 0x0036f7a8)

| 2 |

b (address 0x0036f790)

| 0x0036f7ac |

⊢————————————————————→ arr[1] (address 0x0036f7ac)

| 2 |

This is because, *a = *b turns into *(0x0036f7a8) = *(0x0036f7ac) which is equivalent to arr[0] = arr[1]. Basically, *a access the content of the address stored in a while a is just the address stored in a.

The final example shows pass by reference on pointers.

```cpp
#include <iostream>
using namespace std;

int main()
{
    int number = 7;
    int*   a = &number;
    int* &b = a; // Pass by Reference (b is another name of a)     (1)

    *a = 10;                                                    // (2)
    cout << "number is: " << number << endl;
    cout << "Address of a: " << a << endl;
    cout << "Content of the address in a: " << *a << endl;
    cout << "Address of b: " << b << endl;
    cout << "Content of the address in b: " << *b << endl;

    *b = 11;                                                    // (3)
    cout << "number is: " << number << endl;
    cout << "Address of a: " << a << endl;
    cout << "Content of the address in a: " << *a << endl;
    cout << "Address of b: " << b << endl;
    cout << "Content of the address in b: " << *b << endl;

    int number2nd = 100;
    a = &number2nd;                                             // (4)

    cout << "number2nd is: " << number2nd << endl;
    cout << "Address of a: " << a << endl;
    cout << "Content of the address in a: " << *a << endl;
    cout << "Address of b: " << b << endl;
    cout << "Content of the address in b: " << *b << endl;
}
```

When the program finished executing (1), below is what the pointers look like. Both a and b point to number. a is just an alias of b.

a (address 0x0035fd74)

| 0x0035fd80 |

⊢————————————————————→ number (address 0x0035fd80)

| 7 |

b (address 0x0035fd74)

| 0x0035fd80 |

⊢————————————————————→ number (address 0x0035fd80)

| 7 |

a is just an alias of b.

When the program finished executing (2) *(0x0035fd80) = 10, below is what the pointers look like. Both a and b point to number. a is just an alias of b.

a (address 0x0035fd74)

| 0x0035fd80 |

⊢————————————————————→ number (address 0x0035fd80)

| 10 |

b (address 0x0035fd74)

| 0x0035fd80 |

⊢————————————————————→ number (address 0x0035fd80)

| 10 |

When the program finished executing (3) *(0x0035fd80) = 11, below is what the pointers look like. Both a and b point to number. a is just an alias of b.

a (address 0x0035fd74)

| 0x0035fd80 |

⊢————————————————————→ number (address 0x0035fd80)

| 11 |

b (address 0x0035fd74)

| 0x0035fd80 |

⊢————————————————————→ number (address 0x0035fd80)

| 11 |

When the program finished executing (4) a = &number2nd; => store the address of number2nd to a (since b is the alias of a, b will see the same changes), below is what the pointers look like. Both a and b point to number2nd. a is just an alias of b.

a (address 0x0035fd74)

0x0035fd5c

├─────────────────────────────────►   number2nd (address 0x0035fd5c)

100

b (address 0x0035fd74)

0x0035fd5c

├─────────────────────────────────►   number2nd (address 0x0035fd5c)

100

Practice 9 – Struct and Class

Problem 9.1: What is the output of the program below given the inputs?
123456
105000
Software Engineer

```cpp
#include <iostream>
#include <string>
using namespace std;

struct employee    // we can replace struct by class, but…
{
    int ID;
    double salary;
    string jobtitle;
};    // ← Remember to put semicolon here….

int main()
{
    employee emp;

    cout << "Please enter employee information:\n";

    cout << "ID Number: ";
    cin >> emp.ID;

    cout << "Salary: ";
    cin >> emp.salary; cin.ignore(1000,'\n');

    cout << "Job title: ";
    getline(cin,emp.jobtitle);

    cout << "There is one employee:\n";

    cout << "ID Number: " << emp.ID << endl;
    cout << "Salary: " << emp.salary << endl;
    cout << "Job Title: " << emp.jobtitle << endl;
}
```

Problem 9.2: What is the output of the program below given the inputs?
123456
105000
Software Engineer

```cpp
#include <iostream>
#include <string>
using namespace std;

struct employee // Can we replace struct by class?
{
    int ID;
    double salary;
    string jobtitle;
};

int main()
{
    employee emp_a;
    employee *emp = &emp_a;

    // The arrow, ->, is used with a pointer to acess the members
    // of a struct/class.    emp->ID is equivalent to (*emp).ID

    cout << "ID Number: ";
    cin >> emp->ID;

    cout << "Salary: ";
    cin >> (*emp).salary;

    cin.ignore(1000,'\n');
    cout << "Job title: ";
    getline(cin,emp->jobtitle);

    cout << "There is one employee:\n";
    cout << "ID Number: " << emp->ID << endl;
    cout << "Salary: " << emp->salary << endl;
    cout << "Job Title: " << emp->jobtitle << endl;
}
```

Problem 9.3: What is the output of the program below given the inputs?
123456
105000
Software Engineer

```cpp
#include <iostream>
#include <string>
using namespace std;

struct employee // Can we replace struct by class?
{
    int ID;
    double salary;
    string jobtitle;
};
void getInput(employee emp)    // Should this be "employee &emp" ?
{
    cout << "ID Number: ";
    cin >> emp.ID;

    cout << "Salary: ";
    cin >> emp.salary;

    cin.ignore(1000,'\n');
    cout << "Job title: ";
    getline(cin,emp.jobtitle);
}
int main()
{
    employee emp = {0,0,""};   // initialization
    // same as: emp.ID = 0; emp.salary = 0; emp.jobtitle = "";

    getInput(emp);

    cout << "There are 1 employee:\n";

    cout << "ID Number: " << emp.ID << endl;
    cout << "Salary: " << emp.salary << endl;
    cout << "Job Title: " << emp.jobtitle << endl;
}
```

Problem 9.4: What is the output of the program below given the inputs?
123456
105000
Software Engineer
246802
130000
Senior Software Engineer

```cpp
#include <iostream>
#include <string>
using namespace std;

struct employee // Can we replace struct by class?
{
    int ID;
    double salary;
    string jobtitle;
};

int main()
{
    employee emp[2];
    // employee *emp = new employee[2];

    for(int i=0;i<2;i++)
    {   cout << "ID Number: "; cin >> emp[i].ID;
        cout << "Salary: ";      cin >> emp[i].salary; cin.ignore(1000,'\n');
        cout << "Job title: "; getline(cin,emp[i].jobtitle);
    }

    cout << "There are 2 employees:\n";

    for(int i=0;i<2;i++)
    {
        cout << "Employee #" << i+1 << ":" << endl;
        cout << "ID Number: " << emp[i].ID << endl;
        cout << "Salary: " << emp[i].salary << endl;
        cout << "Job Title: " << emp[i].jobtitle << endl;
    }
}
```

Problem 9.5: What is the output of the program below given the inputs?
123456
105000
Software Engineer
246802
130000
Senior Software Engineer

```cpp
#include <iostream>
#include <string>
using namespace std;
struct employee // Can we replace struct by class?
{
    int ID;
    double salary;
    string jobtitle;
};
// same as employee *emp or employee emp[]
void getInput(employee emp[2])
{
    for(int i=0;i<2;i++)
    {   cout << "ID Number: ";  cin >> emp[i].ID;
        cout << "Salary: ";     cin >> emp[i].salary; cin.ignore(1000,'\n');
        cout << "Job title: ";  getline(cin,emp[i].jobtitle);
    }
}
int main()
{
    employee emp[2];

    getInput(emp);

    cout << "There are 2 employees:\n";
    for(int i=0;i<2;i++)
    {
        cout << "Employee #" << i+1 << ":" << endl;
        cout << "ID Number: " << emp[i].ID << endl;
        cout << "Salary: " << emp[i].salary << endl;
        cout << "Job Title: " << emp[i].jobtitle << endl;
    }
}
```

Problem 9.6: What is the output of the program below?

```cpp
#include <iostream>
#include <string>
using namespace std;

struct employee // Can we replace struct by class?
{
public:
    void outputID() { cout << ID << endl; }
    int ID;
    double salary;
};

int main()
{
    employee emp[5];

    // Before we rotate left at the first position

    for(int i = 0 ; i < 5 ; i++ )
    {
        emp[i].ID = i;
        emp[i].salary = 10000*i + 50000;
        emp[i].outputID();
    }

    cout << "====" << endl;

    // Now we want to rotate left at the first position

    employee temp = emp[0];
    for(int i = 0 ; i < 4 ; i++ )
        emp[i] = emp[i + 1];
    emp[4] = temp;

    for(int i = 0 ; i < 5 ; i++ )
        emp[i].outputID();
}
```

Problem 9.7: What is the output of the program below given the inputs?
123456
105000
Software Engineer

```cpp
#include <iostream>
#include <string>
using namespace std;
class employee
{
public:
    void input();          // public member function
    void output();         // public member function
private:
    int ID;                // private data member
    double salary;         // private data member
    string jobtitle;       // private data member
};
void employee::input()
{
    cout << "ID Number: ";
    cin >> ID;
    cout << "Salary: ";
    cin >> salary; cin.ignore(1000,'\n');
    cout << "Job title: ";
    getline(cin,jobtitle);
}
void employee::output()
{
    cout << "There is one employee:\n";
    cout << "ID Number: " << ID << endl;
    cout << "Salary: " << salary << endl;
    cout << "Job Title: " << jobtitle << endl;
}
int main()
{
    employee emp;

    emp.input();
    emp.output();
}
```

Problem 9.8: If the following program doesn't compile, why not? If it does compile, what is the output of the program below given the inputs?
123456
105000
Software Engineer

```cpp
#include <iostream>
#include <string>
using namespace std;

class employee
{
    int ID;
    double salary;
    string jobtitle;
};

int main()
{
    employee *emp = new employee;
    // This also works: employee *emp = new employee();

    cout << "ID Number: ";
    cin >> emp->ID;
    cout << "Salary: ";
    cin >> (*emp).salary;
    cin.ignore(1000,'\n');
    cout << "Job title: ";
    getline(cin,emp->jobtitle);

    cout << "There is one employee:\n";

    cout << "ID Number: " << emp->ID << endl;
    cout << "Salary: " << emp->salary << endl;
    cout << "Job Title: " << emp->jobtitle << endl;
}
```

Problem 9.9: What is the output of the program below?

```cpp
#include <iostream>
#include <string>
using namespace std;

struct employee
{
    int ID;
    double salary;
    string jobtitle;
};

int main()
{
    employee   emp1[2];
    // An employee struct array with 2 cells.
    // Each cell is an employee object.

    employee *emp2 = new employee[2];
    // An employee* pointer points to the starting address of the
    // Employee struct array with 2 cells

    employee *emp3[2];
    // emp3[0] stores an employee struct pointer (points to a random place)
    // emp3[1] also points to a random place.

    cout << "Static array: size = " << sizeof(emp1[0]) << endl;

    cout << "Dynamic array: size = " << sizeof(emp2[0]) << endl;

    cout << "Array storing only pointers: size = "
        << sizeof(emp3[0])    << endl;
}
```

Problem 9.10: If the following program doesn't compile, why not? If it does compile, what is the output when it is run?

```cpp
#include <iostream>
#include <string>
using namespace std;

class employee
{
public:
    employee()
    {
        ID=0;
        salary=0;
        jobtitle="";
    }
    employee(int ID, double salary, string jobtitle)
    {
        this->ID = ID;
        this->salary = salary;
        this->jobtitle = jobtitle;
    }

    ~employee()
    {
        cout << "This is destructor!!" << endl;
    }
    void Output();
private:
    int ID;
    double salary;
    string jobtitle;
};

void employee::Output()
{
    cout << "ID Number: " << ID << endl;
    cout << "Salary: " << salary << endl;
    cout << "Job Title: " << jobtitle << endl;
}
```

```cpp
int main()
{
    employee A;                                              // (1)

    employee B();                                            // (2)

    employee C = {0,0,""};                                   // (3)

    employee D(1234, 90000.0, "Software Engineer");          // (4)

    employee *E = new employee;                              // (5)

    employee *F = new employee();                            // (6)

    employee *G = new employee(5432, 95000.0, "Manager");    // (7)

    A.Output();                                              // (8)

    B.Output();                                              // (9)

    C.Output();                                              // (10)

    D.Output();                                              // (11)

    E->Output();                                             // (12)

    F->Output();                                             // (13)

    G->Output();                                             // (14)
}
```

```cpp
// The general way to code a class is to
// (1) Hide information: leave data member in private section
// (2) Declare accessor and mutator functions to access private members.
//         - Accessor: only read the private data members out.
//         - Mutator: change the private data members.

#include <iostream>
#include <string>
using namespace std;

class employee
{
public:
    // Is it okay NOT to declare your own constructor and destructor?

    void setValues(int theID, double theSalary)
    {     // This is a mutator function
        ID = theID; salary = theSalary;
    }

    // These two member functions below are accessor functions
    int getID()
    {
        return ID;
    }
    double getSalary();

private:
    int ID;
    double salary;
};

double employee::getSalary()
{
    return salary;
}
```

```cpp
int main()
{
    employee emp[2];

    emp[0].setValues(1, 100000.0);
    emp[1].setValues(2, 110000.0);

    cout << "ID1: "        << emp[0].getID()
        << " Salary1 = "   << emp[0].getSalary() << endl;

    cout << "ID2: "        << emp[1].getID()
        << " Salary2 = "   << emp[1].getSalary() << endl;
}
```

```cpp
#include <iostream>
#include <string>
using namespace std;
class employee
{
public:
    employee()
    {
        ID=0;
        salary=0;
        jobtitle="";
    }

    void setData(int ID, double salary, string jobtitle)
    {
        this->ID = ID;
        this->salary = salary;
        this->jobtitle = jobtitle;
    }

    int getID() const {    return ID;    }

    ~employee()
    {
        cout << ID << " got laid off!!" << endl;
    }

    void Output() {
        cout << "ID Number: " << ID << endl;
        cout << "Salary: " << salary << endl;
        cout << "Job Title: " << jobtitle << endl;
    }

private:
    int ID;
    double salary;
    string jobtitle;
};
```

```cpp
class company
{
public:
    company() { }
    company(string name,int numEmp)
    {
        this->name = name;
        emp = new employee[numEmp];
        for(int i=0;i<numEmp;i++)
        {
            emp[i].setData(i+1, 80000,"Software Engineer");
            cout << emp[i].getID()
                << " got hired to join the company" << endl;
        }
    }
    ~company()
    {
        cout << this->name << " company goes bankrupt!!" << endl;
        delete [] emp;
    }
private:
    employee *emp;
    string name;
};

int main()
{
    company comp("ABC", 2);
}
```

Practice 9 – Solution

9.1:   There is one employee:
ID Number: 123456
Salary: 105000
Job Title: Software Engineer

9.2:   There is one employee:
ID Number: 123456
Salary: 105000
Job Title: Software Engineer

9.3:   There are 1 employee:
ID Number: 0
Salary: 0
Job Title:
Note: the getInput() function should take as input the argument
"employee &emp" to pass by reference, so that the values obtained from the
user inputs can be stored to the correct struct variable.

9.4:   There are 2 employees:
Employee #1:
ID Number: 123456
Salary: 105000
Job Title: Software Engineer
Employee #2:
ID Number: 246802
Salary: 130000
Job Title: Senior Software Engineer

9.5:   There are 2 employees:
Employee #1:
ID Number: 123456
Salary: 105000
Job Title: Software Engineer
Employee #2:
ID Number: 246802
Salary: 130000
Job Title: Senior Software Engineer

9.6:   0
1
2
3
4
====
1
2
3
4
0

152

9.7: There is one employee:
ID Number: 123456
Salary: 105000
Job Title: Software Engineer

9.8: Compilation error because ID, salary, jobtitle data members are not accessible from outside employee object as they are private data members. To resolve this issue, use the public keyword like:

```
class employee
{
public:
    int ID;
    double salary;
    string jobtitle;
};
```

9.9: <u>Note:</u> you should see different values on different machines
* In GCC 4.8.4 on Ubuntu 14.04 64-bit machine:
Static array: size = 24
Dynamic array: size = 24
Array storing only pointers: size = 8
* In Visual C++ 2015 on Windows 7 32-bit machine:
Static array: size = 48
Dynamic array: size = 48
Array storing only pointers: size = 4
* The idea is to show the difference in sizes between the array of pointers and the array of objects.

9.10: In C++11, (9) causes a compilation error because (2) is to declare the prototype of a function B taking 0 arguments and returning an employee object. In other words, the compiler thinks that the function implementation for the function B is after the main() function like:

```
int main()
{
    employee B(); // the prototype of the function B
}
employee B()        // the implementation of the function B
{
    employee b;
    return b;
}
```

Thus, B is not an object, so it cannot use B.Output().

9.11: ID1: 1 Salary1 = 100000
ID2: 2 Salary2 = 110000
<u>Note:</u> If you do not declare any constructor / destructor, then the C++ compiler will make default constructor(s) / destructor for you. If you declare a constructor/destructor, then C++ compiler will not make a default one for you.

9.12: 1 got hired to join the company
2 got hired to join the company
ABC company goes bankrupt!!
2 got laid off!!
1 got laid off!!

Practice Final Exam

Problem	Maximal Possible Points	Received
1	60	
2	10	
3	10	
4	10	
5	10	
6	10	
7	10	
8	15	
9	15	
Total Score	150	

Problem #1: There is a Vending Machine Class called VM below. Please complete the codes under the comment TODO. The output of this program is:

I bought Coke
Pepsi is sold out!!

```
#include <iostream>
#include <string>
using namespace std;
const int MAXSODA = 100;

class Soda
{
public:
    Soda();
    void setName(string name);
    string getName() const;
private:
    string name;
};

Soda::Soda()
{
    // TODO: set name = "NA" to signal Not Available (5 points)


}
void Soda::setName(string name)
{
    // TODO: set Soda's name as the name passed in. (5 points)


}
string Soda::getName() const
{
    // TODO: return Soda's name. (5 points)


}
```

```
class VM
{
public:
    VM(int n);
    ~VM();
    void restock(string name,int quantity);
    Soda* getSoda(string name);
    bool buySoda(string name);
private:
    Soda* inventory[MAXSODA];
    int quantity[MAXSODA];
    int numSoda;
};

VM::VM(int n)
{
    numSoda = n;

    for(int i=0;i<numSoda;i++)
        inventory[ i ] = new Soda();
}

VM::~VM()
{
    // TODO: (10 points)
    // Delete the storage pointed to by Soda pointers in inventory array



}
```

```cpp
void VM::restock(string name,int quantity)
{
    for(int i=0;i<numSoda;i++)
        if( inventory[i]->getName() == "NA")
        {
            // TODO: (10 points)
            // 1. If we found a Soda that has the name "NA", we set
            //     this Soda to have the name we passed into this
            function.
            // 2. Set the quantity for that Soda.
            // 3. Break out of this loop.




        }
}


Soda* VM::getSoda(string name)
{

    // TODO: (10 points)
    // Search all Soda Objects to see if there's a matching Soda by name
    //      If there is a matching soda by name, return that Soda object.
    //      Return nullptr if there's no matching Soda by name.








}
```

```cpp
bool VM::buySoda(string name)
{
    // TODO: (15 points)
    // 1. Search through all Soda objects to find matching Soda by name
    //        If there is a matching soda by name, and if the quantity is > 0.
    //        then we decrease quantity for the Soda by 1 and return true
    //        If there is a matching soda by name, but the quantity is <= 0
    //        then we return false.
    //        If there is no matching soda name, return false.




}

int main()
{
    VM vm(5);
    vm.restock("Coke",4);
    vm.restock("Diet Coke",5);
    vm.restock("Sprite",1);
    vm.restock("Pepsi",0);
    vm.restock("Lemonade",1);

    if (vm.buySoda("Coke"))
        cout << "I bought " << vm.getSoda("Coke")->getName() << endl;
    else
        cout << "Coke is sold out!!" << endl;

    if (vm.buySoda("Pepsi"))
        cout << "I bought " << vm.getSoda("Pepsi")->getName() << endl;
    else
        cout << "Pepsi is sold out!!" << endl;
}
```

Problem #2: Given two strings str1 and str2, str1 is the permutation of str2 if all the characters in str1 appear in str2 but in different order. For example, "12345" is the permutation of "54132". Assume that only '1' – '9' will appear in the string. A student coded the following program to solve this problem, but there are something wrong. Please find all the bugs in this program.

```cpp
#include <iostream>
#include <string>
using namespace std;

bool isPermutation(string str1, string str2)
{
    if(str1.size() != str2.size())
        return false;

    int i, j, counts[10];

    for(i=0;i<10;i++)
        counts[i] = 0;

    for(i=0;i<str1.size();i++)
        counts[ str1[i] -    0    ] ++;         // (1)

    for(i=0;i<str1.size();i++)
        counts[ str2[i] -    0    ] --;         // (2)

    for(i=0;i<10;i++)                           // (3)
        if(counts[i] != 0)                      // (4)
            return true;                        // (5)
    return false;                               // (6)
}
```

```
int main()
{
    cout << isPermutation("ABCDE", "BDECA") << endl;
    cout << isPermutation("BALLS", "CALLS") << endl;
}
```

The bugs are in?
(A) 123456
(B) 12356
(C) 1256
(D) 234
(E) 2356
(F) 256
(G) 356
(H) 3
(I) 12
(J) 34

Problem #3: A student implemented a function called deleteB(char *msg) to delete all the B in a C-string. Can you please help evaluate his codes below and tell him what is the output of this program?

```cpp
#include <iostream>
using namespace std;

void deleteB(char *msg)
{
    char *ptr;
    while(*msg != 0)
    {
        if(*msg =='B' || *msg =='b')
        {
            ptr = msg;

            while (*ptr != 0)
            {
                *ptr=*( ptr + 1 );
                ptr++;
            }
        }
        msg++;
    }
}

int main()
{
    char msg[100] = "BaabbaBaB";
    deleteB(msg);
    cout << msg;
}
```

(1) aaaa
(2) aabaa
(3) BaaaaB
(4) BabaBaB
(5) aabbaa
(6) aaaaB
(7) Baaaa
(8) aaaBa

Problem #4: What is the output of the program below?

```cpp
#include <iostream>
#include <string>
using namespace std;
int foo( string s )
{
    if (s.size () < 1)
        return -1;

    int mult = 1;
    int offs = 0;
    switch (s[0])
    {
        case '-':
            mult = -1;
            break ;
        case '+':
            mult = 1;
            break ;
        default :
            offs = 1;
            break ;
    }
    return mult * (s[1 - offs ] - '0');
}

int foo2(string exp)
{
    string exp1="", exp2="", exp3="";
    int i;

    for(i=0;i<=1;i++) exp1 += exp[i];
    for(i=5;i<=7;i++) exp2 += exp[i];
    for(i=8;i<=13;i++) exp3 += exp[i];

    return foo(exp1) + foo(exp2) + foo(exp3);
}
```

```
int main()
{
    cout << foo2("-3+3+555+99999") << endl;
    return 0;
}
```

(A) 1
(B) 2
(C) 3
(D) 4
(E) 5
(F) 6
(G) 7
(H) 8
(I) 9
(J) 10
(K) 11
(L) 12

Problem #5: Below is a zurt class definition. In the main function, we declare a const Zurt * pointer pointing to a zurt object. At the <BLANK> below, which member functions can we call without causing compilation error? For example, can we use zp−>health(); ? There are more than one answers to this question. Please find all the answers.

```cpp
#include <iostream>
using namespace std;
class Zurt
{
public:
    Zurt() { m_health = m_row = m_col = 0; }
    Zurt(int health, int r,int c) {
        m_health = health;
        m_row = r;   m_col = c;
    }
    int health() const { return m_health; }
    int row() const { return m_row; }
    int col() const { return m_col; }
    void setHealth(int health) { m_health = health; }
    void setRow(int r) { m_row = r; }
    void setCol(int c) { m_col = c; }
private:
    int m_health, m_row, m_col;
};

int main()
{
    Zurt z(100,1,1);
    const Zurt* zp = &z;

    <BLANK>

    return 0;
}
```

(A) zp−>Zurt();   (B) zp−>Zurt(100,1,2);   (C) int h = zp−>health();
(D) int r = zp−>row();   (E) int c = zp−>col();   (F) zp−>setHealth(50);
(G) zp−>setRow(2);   (H) zp−>setCol(2);   (I) zp−>m_col = 5;

Problem #6: Below is a zurt class definition. In the main function, we declare a Zurt * pointer pointing to a zurt object. At the <BLANK> below, which member functions can we call without causing compilation error? For example, can we use zp−>health(); ? There are more than one answers to this question. Please find all the answers. Please note that this problem is slightly different from problem #5.

```
#include <iostream>
using namespace std;
class Zurt
{
public:
    Zurt() { m_health = m_row = m_col = 0; }
    Zurt(int health, int r,int c) {
        m_health = health;
        m_row = r;   m_col = c;
    }
    int health() const { return m_health; }
    int row() const { return m_row; }
    int col() const { return m_col; }
    void setHealth(int health) { m_health = health; }
    void setRow(int r) { m_row = r; }
    void setCol(int c) { m_col = c; }
private:
    int m_health, m_row, m_col;
};

int main()
{
    Zurt z(100,1,1);
    Zurt* zp = &z;

    <BLANK>

    return 0;
}
```
(A) zp−>Zurt();   (B)   zp−>Zurt(100,1,2);   (C) int h = zp−>health();
(D) int r = zp−>row();   (E) int c = zp−>col();   (F) zp−>setHealth(50);
(G) zp−>setRow(2);   (H) zp−>setCol(2); (I) zp−>m_col = 5;

Problem #7: What is the output of the program below?

```cpp
#include <iostream>
using namespace std;
int main()
{
    int arr[12] = {1,3,5,0,7,2,0,4,4,0,8,8};
    int count = 0;
    for(int i=0;i<11;i++) {
        if(arr[i] = arr[i+1] )
            count++;
        else
            count--;
    }
    cout << count << endl;
}
```

Problem #8: What is the output of the program below?

```cpp
#include <iostream>
using namespace std;
int main()
{
    int arr[100] = {1,1,2,3,5,8};
    int *p = (arr+6);
    for(int i=0;i<2;i++) {
        *p = *(p-1) + *(p-2);
        p++;
    }
    cout << *(p-1) << endl;
}
```

```cpp
#include <iostream>
using namespace std;

void swap2(int* a, int *b)
{
    int temp = *a;
    *a = *b;
    *b = temp;
}

int main()
{
    int arr[7] = { 2,4,6,8,1,3,5 };
    int* first = arr;
    int* last = arr+6;
    int divider = 4;

    while(first < last)
    {
        while( (first < last) && (*first < divider) )
            first++;
        while( (first < last) && (*last   > divider) )
            last--;
        swap2(first,last);
    }

    for(first = arr ; first < arr+7; first++)
        cout << *first << " ";
    cout << endl;
}
```

Practice Final Exam – Solution

1:

```cpp
#include <iostream>
#include <string>
using namespace std;
const int MAXSODA = 100;

class Soda
{
public:
    Soda();
    void setName(string name);
    string getName() const;
private:
    string name;
};

Soda::Soda()
{
    // TODO: set name = "NA" to signal Not Available (5 points)
    this->name = "NA";
}

void Soda::setName(string name)
{
    // TODO: set Soda's name as the name passed in. (5 points)
    this->name = name;
    // We have to use this->name here.
}

string Soda::getName() const
{
    // TODO: return Soda's name. (5 points)
    return name;
    // or return this->name;
}

class VM
{
public:
    VM(int n);
    ~VM();
    void restock(string name, int quantity);
    Soda* getSoda(string name);
    bool buySoda(string name);
private:
    Soda* inventory[MAXSODA];
    int quantity[MAXSODA];
    int numSoda;
};

VM::VM(int n)
{
    numSoda = n;

    for (int i = 0; i<numSoda; i++)
        inventory[i] = new Soda();
}
```

```cpp
VM::~VM()
{
    // TODO: (10 points)
    // Delete the storage pointed to by Soda pointers in inventory array
    for (int i = 0; i<numSoda; i++)
        delete inventory[i];
}

void VM::restock(string name, int quantity)
{
    for (int i = 0; i<numSoda; i++)
        if (inventory[i]->getName() == "NA")
        {
            // TODO: (10 points)
            // 1. If we found a Soda that has the name "NA", we set
            // this Soda to have the name we passed into this function.
            // 2. Set the quantity for that Soda.
            // 3. Break out of this loop.
            inventory[i]->setName(name);

            this->quantity[i] = quantity;

            break;    // or return;
        }
}

Soda* VM::getSoda(string name)
{
    // TODO: (10 points)
    // Search all Soda Objects to see if there's a matching Soda by name
    //      If there is a matching soda by name, return that Soda object.
    //      Return nullptr if there's no matching Soda by name.

    for (int i = 0; i<numSoda; i++)
        if (inventory[i]->getName() == name)
            return inventory[i];
    return nullptr;
}

bool VM::buySoda(string name)
{
    // TODO: (15 points)
    // 1. Search through all Soda objects to find matching Soda by name
    //      If there is a matching soda by name, and if the quantity is>0.
    //      then we decrease quantity for the Soda by 1 and return true
    //      If there is a matching soda by name, but the quantity is <= 0
    //      then we return false.
    //      If there is no matching soda name, return false.

    for (int i = 0; i<numSoda; i++)
        if (inventory[i]->getName() == name && quantity[i] > 0)
        {
            quantity[i]--;
            return true;
        }
    return false;
}
```

```
int main()
{
    VM vm(5);
    vm.restock("Coke", 4);
    vm.restock("Diet Coke", 5);
    vm.restock("Sprite", 1);
    vm.restock("Pepsi", 0);
    vm.restock("Lemonade", 1);

    if (vm.buySoda("Coke"))
        cout << "I bought " << vm.getSoda("Coke")->getName() << endl;
    else
        cout << "Coke is sold out!!" << endl;

    if (vm.buySoda("Pepsi"))
        cout << "I bought " << vm.getSoda("Pepsi")->getName() << endl;
    else
        cout << "Pepsi is sold out!!" << endl;
}
```

2:   (C)
(1) Should be counts[str1[i]- '0']++;
(2) Should be counts[str2[i]- '0']--;
(5) Should be return false;
(6) Should be return true;

3:   (2)

4:   (K)

5:   (C)(D)(E)

6:   (C)(D)(E)(F)(G)(H)

7:   5

8:   21

9:   2 3 1 4 8 6 5

Made in the USA
Monee, IL
08 January 2025